I GOT UP

I GOT UP

A Mother's Story of Grief, Resilience, and Unending Love

BY BRENDA DALY

Published and distributed by Soul Speak Press
Virginia, USA

Library of Congress Control Number: 2024910876

Daly, Brenda
I Got Up: A Mother's Story of Grief, Resilience, and Unending Love

Cover design by Genevieve Bryan of Paper Panther Studio.

ISBN 978-1-958472-19-4 - Paperback
978-1-958472-20-0 eBook

To Kevin
Forever in our hearts.

Contents

Foreword

About a year ago, Brenda Daly and I were connected by a mutual friend because we had one big thing in common: traumatic brain injury (TBI). My relationship with TBI is from my own lived experience, while hers was through the story of her son Kevin. My TBI was sustained from a bicycle accident in 2011, and it turned my world upside down. Over the next decade, I was fortunate enough to be able to unearth enough resilience to start climbing up and out of the hole that TBI causes for many of those unfortunate enough to experience it. It's a type of climb no amount of life experience can prepare you for.

As I learned how to manage my symptoms and struggles, my challenges remained a mystery to everyone else because of the most frustrating and debilitating result of all—the invisibility factor. Kevin and I "looked fine" on the outside, resulting in expectations for us to return to "normal" and perform the same way we used to. That is a typical story after a brain injury. And an impossibility.

Through my roles as a brain injury coach, public speaker, best-selling author, advocate, and educator, I have had the incredible opportunity to connect with thousands of people on the aftereffects of living with a brain injury. Even with all the work I have been able to do in coordination with others, it is very clear that there is still much education and awareness needed to reduce the stigma around brain injury survivors, and to do that, we must understand the chronic nature of this condition. Being aware of the sometimes worst-case scenario endings is something no one wants to do, but a must, nonetheless. With Brenda's book, the gap in understanding will have closed a little more.

Looking back, I can see that what grabbed my attention the first time I talked to Brenda is the same thing that comes through clearly in this book; she has a type of learned wisdom and innate determination that only comes from an experience as profound as hers. Watching and responding to a loved one with a very ambiguous condition changes a person. While life can be hard and overwhelming at times, *I Got Up* tells the most extreme and overwhelming version you can imagine. Even more so, the fact that after years of watching her son suffer, after so much fruitless advocating and lost nights worrying that then morphed into unimaginable grief, Brenda somehow had enough strength left inside of her to get up and keep going. The radius of impact that Kevin's journey had on his mother and their entire family is amply illustrated. Brenda's plight was to find support from clinicians and doctors. She begged for help for her son. What she found was something different.

I didn't want to stop reading Brenda's heartfelt and compelling tribute to her son. Her journey's ups, downs, and length are a testament to the parent's role when their child is ill or injured. Brenda sheds light on well-intentioned but ignorant actions and comments from others that caused further physical and emotional distress after her son's accident. She also recounts numerous errors that led her son, and their family, to become victims due to uninformed medical professionals and understaffed medical facilities. As an author, Brenda generously leads us through a terrible sequence of events that occurs when you take to the streets for help when the medical world quite simply just doesn't believe your pain.

Even with the many complex themes in this book, the one thing shining through is the author's legacy to her son's spirit and her love and dedication to fighting for his survival in personal, professional, emotional, and physical realms.

I can assure the reader from my own experience that brain injury is not an easy condition to live with. The medical journey is time-consuming and frustrating, to say the very least. The losses are profound and unexpected. I myself have lost friends, family members, and my career. I have had to pick myself up and carry my traumatized brain back to a place where I could rebuild my self-esteem and establish a new identity. It's no wonder that so many survivors live day after day with unrest, fear, and hopelessness, which can lead to more and more despair over time.

Even though Brenda doesn't have a brain injury, *I Got Up* validated parts of my own journey through her astute observations from the hours of her life that were dedicated to her son's recovery. What she can offer that supersedes brain injuries and their aftermath is the long and unforgiving journey of grief. Brenda's insights reached my core as someone who "gets it." And anyone else will relate to this work because this story is ultimately one of love, loss, grief, and finding purpose when so much of your love is gone.

It's not easy, no. But through these pages, Brenda proves that even in the depths of indescribable pain and loss, it is possible to get up.

She did.

I did.

And I hope you feel empowered to do so too.

Stacia Bissell, M.Ed.

Introduction

My greatest fear in life as a mother was losing one of my children. I watched with distant curiosity when other mothers suffered the loss of a child. *I couldn't ever get up again if I lost one of my children*, I decided when watching an interview with the parents of a murdered child from the Sandy Hook Elementary School shooting.

How do they go on?

Nothing prepares you for the loss of one of your children. It goes against the natural order of life. Parents die first. That's the way it is designed. I assumed this would be true for me, just like most parents do.

My world shattered into a million pieces on October 21, 2018, when my oldest son died suddenly and unexpectedly. I was knocked down to the ground. At the time, I didn't think I would ever get up again. I didn't know how I would breathe. Life became dark as crushing pain took over. I was devastated. I had no hope for the future as grief screamed into my face like a drill sergeant on the first day of duty. It was relentless; I was powerless in its intensity.

Though I have written a few thousand of my own words for this book, the ending of "Funeral Blues" (also called "Stop All the Clocks") by W. H. Auden is the best description of my early grief:

The stars are not wanted now; put out every one,
Pack up the moon and dismantle the sun,
Pour away the ocean and sweep up the wood;
For nothing now can ever come to any good.

I could never imagine losing my son, and yet I did. And in the aftermath, I could not imagine there was a world available where I would ever feel anything other than sadness and pain for the rest of my life. On days when I was at my worst, I tried to calculate how many years I would have to live without him. Out of curiosity, people will ask how my son Kevin died, and when I answer honestly, that it was partly because of fentanyl, they immediately jump to conclusions. Every single time it's as if I can see the wheels in their brains turning as they picture an addict, a man out of control, someone who should have known better than to take a pill from a friend. They view him through the lens of judgment. Unfairly, that decision to take a pill becomes the most defining moment in the lives of those who die from fentanyl. But, they are much more than their deaths, much more than that one final decision. How Kevin died was only a little piece of his whole life story. There is a lifetime of adventure, love, and pain. So much physical pain that I don't know how he coped with it. In my eyes, he is a hero. It is remarkable that Kevin endured unbearable pain for as long as he did; that he managed successfully for as long as he did. He suffered. Oh yes, there was emotional pain, too, amid marital struggles, and the discrimination he faced daily for his disability and chronic pain problems.

But, all that said, I understand why people react the way they do. Our society stigmatizes people with addiction; most people operate under the misconception that someone's drug or alcohol use is a choice, a weakness, and therefore a moral failing. There is no consideration of other factors, such as addiction being a brain disease, as research indicates. "I would never do that!" they exclaim as they proclaim their moral superiority from a place of privileged ignorance.

Each and every person who dies of fentanyl has a unique story that came to them by way of excruciating circumstances. But we blame them—they made their choice. Yet people like Kevin—and Kevin himself—were loved. They were—they are—mourned. Their families grieve. Their mothers hurt.

I hurt.

So, why did I write this book when it exposes Kevin, and me, to moral judgment? Why am I making myself vulnerable to criticism and negative attitudes from readers as a family member of someone who died with fentanyl in their system? Why reopen the wound and put it in black and white and watch it bleed? Because I want to address the stigma for traumatic brain injuries, chronic pain patients, and substance-involved deaths. I feel compelled to expose the disenfranchised grief; the unacknowledged grief family members suffer because of the stigmatization of a substance-related death. And I want the family members to feel heard and understood. I want to offer hope. But mostly, I want to remember my son.

Even after more than five years have passed, I still ache for my boy. I miss him every day. I have continued to wonder, after the sudden shock of finding his dead body, if it would be possible for me to ever recover.

It turns out that I didn't recover in the traditional sense. I never "healed." I never became whole again. Because when he died, it left me shattered in fragments.

What I did do, however, was something more realistic—and something I once thought was impossible. I got up.

CHAPTER 1

I Got Up

I'm a clinical social worker. A therapist. I'm a feelings-oriented person; I talk about my feelings all the time, and I listen to other people talk about their feelings for a living. But after Kevin died, I was in a different zone. No time for feelings. I had to function. I had to survive for my family, which seemed impossible, while I was trying to put all the shattered pieces together to make myself whole again too. How was I going to do that? I fell back on my training, I looked for resources. I read everything I could about grief. I took courses. I became a certified grief therapist.

It was in one of my many therapy classes, this one focusing on art-assisted grief therapy, that I was given an assignment to create a collage. As part of the training, we were asked to do an experiential exercise using collage to integrate the fragmented pieces we experienced after a loss. We were given the first twenty minutes of the exercise to search through magazines for images that struck us positively or negatively. I leafed through several pages until I landed on a picture of First Lady Jill Biden, clad in a beautiful navy blue suit, standing next to a presidential-style building. She looked strong and was smiling. I immediately recalled an interview I had heard with her where she very candidly expressed her struggles after the loss of her son, and I identified with her during the interview.

As I studied her smiling face, I looked for proof in her eyes that she was actually functioning in the world again. It occurred to me that I was functioning in the world again too. I was struck by her ability to continue standing amid her pain.

I cut her out and put the image aside. I thumbed through another few pages and stopped on a black-and-white picture of a woman lying on dark, hard rocks near the ocean. Though it was a still image, it was as if I could hear the waves crashing in the distance, and I could feel her despair. I noted that she had a bare breast and immediately considered covering her up. She was exposed, raw, vulnerable.

Exactly how I feel, I suddenly realized.

I cut it out and left the picture the way it was, bare breast and all. I continued clipping out images that spoke to me. Then, when our time was up, we were asked to glue the images to a white poster board. I glued Jill Biden on first, she continued her stately stance on the right side of my poster, where I also laid a colorful blue paper for background. On the left, I pasted the woman lying on the rocky shore, with a black background underneath. There was a wide gap in the middle of the two. I studied it, not knowing what to put there.

I found another black-and-white image, this one of a woman standing on a rocky shore, her right arm stretched in a sweeping gesture as if she were letting go of something, leaving something behind. I had torn out this picture since something in me identified with the image. I cleaned the edges and glued it in the middle of the other two pictures. It seemed to fit perfectly.

Everyone in the class then took turns explaining the symbolism in their collages. When my turn came, I explained that I connected with Jill Biden because she was a bereaved mother who was functioning in life and it symbolized how I, too, had begun to return to functioning in my own life, while still grieving my son. The woman lying on the rocks while the waves crashed around her represented me in the early stages of grief. I didn't know if I could ever function again. That first year, I had acute pain. Grief hurts, and there was nothing but sadness and longing in that first stage of loss. I didn't know how I was even breathing. I didn't know how I was going to go on—how was I going to live my life without my son whom I adored so much? There seemed to be no answer. Like the woman slumped in the picture, I had that cold, caved-in feeling, and I was waiting for the sea of grief to swallow me up.

When I got to the third picture, I stopped for a moment to gather myself. I was still processing what this picture meant to me. "This picture represents how I got from the deepest despair to functioning again." I paused and studied the woman standing on the rocks. It struck me like a bolt of lightning as the words came out of my mouth.

"I got up."

And then I began to weep. My tears were quiet and subdued but came from deep within me, from my inner survival.

"I got up," I repeated through my tears, astounded at discovering an element of my resilience in front of all these people. As if the two women in the pictures had become one, I could finally see how I had gone from utter despair to functioning because I got up.

As I gathered myself and wiped my tears, I explained to the group that there were more layers. I had unintentionally divided the collage into black and white on one side, representing the darkness I was mired in at the beginning of my grief, and color on the other side, showing how I could function again. On the picture of Jill Biden, I had added a little red heart that I had torn in two, representing my broken heart. I surrounded it with other red hearts to show that I was still emanating love out into the world, even from a heart that had been torn and shattered into a million pieces. My love for Kevin had not died. My love for my son could never die. My love for Kevin was—and remains to this day—fully alive in my heart. Studying my images, I understood that I had been able to express how I had moved from a state of being caved in on myself, head hanging low, eyes fixed on the ground, to seeing the world in color once again. In just a few magazine cutouts, I was able to represent my entire grief journey: from despair to reengagement of life, from hopelessness to purpose, from black and white to color.

My tears had quieted by this point, but they started up again as I pointed out the last image I had added to my collage, a group of people. Without other bereaved parents, therapists, friends, and family, I explained through my tears, I could not have ever gotten up. It was the people in my life who had picked up piece after piece of my broken heart and helped me put it back together again.

There it was, in black, white, and color, for me to see. Resilience in grief.

It took courage, strength, and connection, but yes, ultimately, I got up.

CHAPTER 2
Growing Up

Motherhood. It brings to mind fantasies about love and marriage for a lot of people. For my generation, tradition teaches us that a girl and boy fall in love, get married, have a baby, and live happily ever after.

That wasn't my story. Is it ever anyone's story? I had the boyfriend part—and not for that long, actually, because after I found out I was pregnant, he was gone. It wasn't that I was unaware of the consequences of having an intimate relationship, but still, I was stunned. *Me? Pregnant?* I couldn't say a word when the doctor told me. I just looked at the test, dumbstruck. I had gone to the medical clinic on the college campus. I was beginning to suspect I might be pregnant but still, I was in denial. The doctor, no doubt, had seen that look many times on many other girls. Once I recovered from the shock and found my voice, the doctor and I discussed my next step. He referred me to a woman at the community mental health clinic to "discuss my options."

Abortions were secretive, but I'm not sure why since it was 1976 and abortion had been legal for about three years. Still, many young women in the small college town in Arizona where I lived were secretly sent by train to California to "take care of the problem," most likely to retain their privacy.

If I were to be taking care of the problem I would be doing so alone. My boyfriend decided he wanted nothing to do with marriage or the responsibility of having a child.

I was twenty.

The counselor I saw at the clinic offered me only one option: abortion. And a train ticket.

"What if I keep the baby?" I asked her.

"What kind of terrible person brings a child into the world without a father?" she barked at me with indignation. "No, your pregnancy is simply a biological mistake."

Biological mistake.

The phrase was cold and empty, emotionally distant. How could the possibility of any child be a mistake? Even if I chose an abortion, wouldn't I grieve? I'd been raised Catholic; it had been drilled into my head that abortion was wrong. It would have been much more useful for me to receive comfort and encouragement from someone like the counselor, instead of her judgment, but once again, I was on my own.

As my belly grew, I'd find myself wandering through bookstores, looking for books that would show me how the baby was developing. The first month showed the baby the size of a grain of sand, a cluster of cells, and then by week three that little cluster of cells begins to take on human characteristics. Page after page I was awestruck at how this seemingly biological mistake was predicted to grow into something the size of a watermelon with a brain and lungs and tiny toes in a matter of months. As I paged through the stages of development, I considered the consequences of my actions. *How do I see this baby? Do I see it as a life?* I was three months along at this point, and when I saw that the baby at three months was the size of a lime that was developing fingernails,

I knew I couldn't go through with an abortion. I knew I was carrying a life and I didn't want to end it.

Each woman finding herself in these circumstances must grapple with her own decisions. I knew myself and I knew I would never be able to reconcile an abortion with my upbringing. My friends helped. They were very supportive of me and my decision. They thought they might have chosen an abortion had they been in my position, but they were adamant I didn't have to.

"Women of our day, we can keep our kids if we want. You can have your baby on your own, Brenda."

When I wavered in my judgment call, I would think about a teacher I adored in high school. She was my psychology teacher—and she was a single parent. I admired her so much. She managed to have a career and raise her children. I even used to babysit for her. And she was thriving. *You can do this*, I would say over and over to myself as my belly bulged.

Because it was my choice.

My choice didn't come without complicated consequences, though, beyond being a single parent, which, obviously, would be hard enough. I couldn't tell my parents—not right away. I remember lying in bed when the realization that I could be completely rejected by my own family for my decision to be an unwed single mother hit me. It was the first time in my life, though not the last, where I would have to dig deep inside myself to stand up for my own values. I wanted to keep this baby—no abortion, no adoption, no secret trains to California— but I also knew what I wanted would not be popular or well-received. I knew it could mean estrangement from my very Catholic family. As the second oldest of ten children, the reality of them rejecting me and my baby was a lot to lose. And still, all the way down to the marrow of my bone, I knew I was making the right choice. And never once have I regretted it.

I GOT UP

The first person I told was my sister Mimi. She's one year older than me, and, at the time, was attending the same college. I was shaking with nerves, but I was also desperate to tell someone. Holding in my secret was excruciating.

"Well," she said when I relayed my news, "I guess we're going to have a baby." Then she handed me a Tootsie Pop.

I cried with relief.

Even though I had managed to tell Mimi, I wasn't brave enough to tell the rest of my family. Not yet anyway. I had moved back home for the summer as I tried to figure out my plan of action. I was very thin, so I didn't look pregnant. Yet, by my fifth month, I was starting to show.

My mother figured it out.

She approached me one day, "Your brother John hears you crying every night." She paused. "It helps to tell someone what's going on."

I trembled. I wanted to; I wanted her love and support and to not feel burdened with this secret anymore, but I was paralyzed with fear of being rejected and ostracized. I just couldn't guess what was on the other side of my revelation: care or condemnation?

"Tell me," Mom said.

So, I did. I cried when I told her I was pregnant, and that I planned to keep the baby. Alone.

She asked about my boyfriend, and I had to explain he was not going to be involved. When we were carefree young adults, life was all about having a good time for him. Yet the reality of being responsible for a baby and having a family to support wasn't something he was mature enough to deal with. Of course, I had the fantasy of love and marriage too. It wasn't exactly the way I wanted to start a family, but I had to let go of my boyfriend. And not just because he was afraid of responsibility. He had become abusive, backhanding me on two different occasions.

The first time was long before I was pregnant when he busted my lip. The second time, he hit me in the eye so hard I threw up. I was pregnant at the time, but neither of us knew it. I knew I had to let go of any notion of this relationship working. Abusive men go after a woman when she is most vulnerable—and now that I was pregnant, I was most definitely vulnerable. That wasn't the life I wanted for me and my baby. I was terrified of what the future would hold; afraid and uncertain, but I decided to keep my eyes focused on what was immediately in front of me—a practice that would serve me well for the rest of my life.

My parents didn't kick me out. They didn't exactly welcome my decision with open arms, though my mother was more supportive than my father at the time, but my worst fears weren't realized, even though it took a long time for my parents to come around.

I was grateful for the care and acceptance they were able to give, but I was wary too. On the one hand, I knew they were probably embarrassed because of the small-town mindset where we lived, but they also didn't want to turn me out on the streets.

My mother was greatly concerned about the example I was setting for my younger siblings. She did not want them to think becoming a single, unwed mother was socially acceptable. Despite it being 1976, people still judged women who decided to keep their baby and raise it alone.

It was a trying time enduring the criticism, listening to my mother's judgment as she explained to my nine- and ten-year-old siblings that my being a single mother was not the right way to do things. I was pregnant and unmarried. Shameful.

I had to enjoy my pregnancy in secret. I would go into the bathroom and stare at my naked body, watching in awe as it bloomed with new life. I would rub my bulge and hold my belly. It was safe in here, no one could shame me—I could feel whatever I wanted in private.

I started to connect to my baby, the doubts disappearing in clouds of love and joy. I read all I could about being a new mother, labor and delivery, and eating healthily for the baby and me. I especially loved

La Leche League's book *The Womanly Art of Breastfeeding*. I never saw my mother nurse any of her children, I just thought people gave babies bottles until one of my girlfriends got pregnant at seventeen and nursed her baby. When I asked her about it, she explained all the reasons it was healthy for mom and baby. I learned about the nursing relationship and the mother-infant bond, and it resonated with me on a deeper level. Nursing was more than feeding a baby; it was nurturing and comforting for both baby and mother. I was so convinced and excited to breastfeed and took that enthusiasm into my Lamaze classes where I learned breathing techniques to assist me in labor. I prepared every day for labor and delivery, though I really didn't have a clue about how painful and difficult it would be.

It was the end of October, and my due date was looming. I had taken a break from college and moved back in with my parents in order to focus on the birth of my baby. My due date came and went with no signs of labor. I remember sitting outside on lawn chairs at my parents' home with my mother and grandmother handing out candy to trick-or-treaters for Halloween. I prayed I wouldn't go into labor on Halloween. I could just see every birthday overshadowed by trick-or-treating. I was a week overdue. I wasn't fully ready for the birth. I had no idea what to expect and only my mother to help me. *What was next?* Reality was setting in. I was excited to meet this little one, but terrified of the responsibility I faced on my own.

The next day, I was in my OB/GYN's office trying not to throw up as he rubbed my cervix in a very determined way. I went home to rest but by the end of the night, as he predicted, I was experiencing severe cramping and bloody show. The baby was coming and there was no stopping it now!

Labor came on aggressively, leaving me little time to think. All my preparation and research did nothing to prepare me for the reality of birthing a human being. Crippled in half, my mother helped me into the car and drove me to the hospital, which was about an hour away from our house. My labor was fast and furious, with contractions starting at two minutes apart. It lasted a total of six hours, and thankfully, my mother was supportive and caring throughout.

I squeezed her hand all the way to the hospital and for most of the labor. When I just didn't think I could take anymore, the nurses asked me if I wanted something for the pain. *Oh my God*, I thought. I couldn't agree fast enough. The pain was nothing like I had prepared for in Lamaze classes. In between drags of breath, I kept thinking, *How come no one told me it was going to hurt this much??* Everyone was advocating for an all-natural birth, but really, who could survive that?

As soon as the pain medication was administered and I gained physical relief, my mind started spinning on how much of a failure I already was to succumb to medication. Message after message from Lamaze classes had been all about empowerment: "Without pain medication—you can do this!" the instructor had chirped.

As I huffed and winced and wondered if my insides were being ripped out, I felt anything but empowered. I couldn't see in that moment that my body was delivering a miracle; breathing at all felt like a miracle.

My mother took one look at me and said only, "Oh, this won't take long." Other women start with contractions twenty minutes apart, perhaps that's what makes labor doable. Why was mine so different? Regardless of my worries, the pain medication helped me relax, and the baby's head appeared.

Kevin arrived after two pushes at around five in the morning on November 2, 1976. Election day. We had a new president, Jimmy Carter. I had a new baby boy. The nurses took my baby away to clean him off before handing him to me as was their protocol at the time; there was no laying the baby on the mother's chest for immediate bonding. I couldn't believe I had a boy. I was so sure I was going to have a girl, I didn't even have a boy's name picked out—not one I was fully invested in at least. I had picked out a girl's name a long time ago and couldn't really imagine myself raising a boy. Then, a nurse arrived at my bedside and handed him over to me.

It was love at first sight.

CHAPTER 3

Love Is All You Need

I remember the first time I laid eyes on Kevin. I fell madly, deeply in love with my sweet baby boy. His birth was an awakening. It was a sudden seismic shift, a movement which was powerful and deeply internal like the earth moving; my heart shifted, it expanded. It filled up. A before and after. In that sterile hospital room, I had experienced a miracle, the miracle of life. Love entered my heart, in a new and beautiful way the moment I held him to me. So precious and innocent, all my instincts came alive as he became my universe. I wanted to love him and protect him. So this was God's gift to the world, love.

Motherhood changed me forever by giving me purpose and clarity. Today, scientists would say it is oxytocin, a hormone released at birth and during nursing, which creates an attachment necessary for survival. For me, it was spiritual and profound. It was the beginning of a lifelong bond that was a mutual love affair. My family fell in love with Kevin too. As I watched my mother cradle him and stare into his sleepy newborn eyes, it was clear he was always meant to be a part of everyone's life. He was most definitely *not* a biological mistake.

Kevin used to say we had a bond—even after his siblings arrived—no one could break. He said it when we were close and when we had an argument. In fact, our last argument was just a few days before he died. I was overwhelmed with the move to the new house we had built and irritated he wasn't helping me more. Kevin was angry with me for expecting extra from him. He had limited resources with his head injury and chronic pain.

As he was leaving the house that day, he shouted back at me, "We have a bond no one can break!" It was true. We had a special bond, a bond that I thought had been severed when he died, until I realized my love for him only and always ever grew, even in death.

I had about a year and a half of coursework left in order to graduate with my bachelor's degree, and finishing college was important to me as a single mother; there was no father in the picture, and I needed a way to provide for my son. Even though they were unwilling to condone my actions of getting pregnant outside of wedlock, my parents did help. I lived at home and commuted for about a year while finishing my undergraduate degree. My mother helped me by caring for Kevin while I went to school or needed time to study.

As Kevin grew, he became close to my younger siblings, almost like a younger brother to them. In the absence of the typical nuclear family, I appreciated that Kevin could experience what it was like to be a part of a big family. It seemed my younger brothers and sisters knew everybody in the small town in Arizona where we lived. They delighted in taking Kevin to be around their friends—younger children don't care how a baby came to be, they just like playing with a new baby. No small-town mindset stopped them. I remember, I'd go to the baseball park and everyone would pass him around. I'd be panicking, *Where's my kid?* And he'd be on the other side of the park.

My sister, Aunt Mimi as Kevin called her, was particularly close to Kevin, having been the first to know about my pregnancy and the most supportive person during my journey. When Kevin was two years old, Mimi was watching him at our town's little league ballpark. My mother was working in the concession stand where Kevin wanted to go get a snack. Mimi picked him up to carry him down the large bleacher steps.

"Wait." He held out his hand to stop. "I want to watch him pitch."

He had his eyes totally focused on the ball players. It was a precursor to the incredible role sports would play in his life, and also the lifelong connection he had to my siblings.

———

By the time he was four, I'd completed my undergraduate degree and had been working for a year. One of my college professors had encouraged me to get my master's degree in social work—I'd been passionate about studying psychology, sociology, and social work since being introduced to psychology by my favorite high school teacher—so I left my job, packed Kevin up, and headed to the big city of Tempe, Arizona, to attend Arizona State University and study for my master's degree in social work. I found an apartment to share with one of my sisters, and I enrolled Kevin in a preschool program near our apartment. I modified my schedule to accommodate being a mother and juggling the responsibilities of an intense master's program. Two days a week, I attended classes all day. Three days a week, I studied, wrote papers, and read material required for classes. Nights and weekends were reserved for Kevin. Summers, when Kevin would return to my parents, I completed my required internships. I wanted to be fully focused on Kevin when he was not in preschool.

The first five years of a child's life are crucial for their development physically, intellectually, and emotionally. Social skills, cognitive skills, and decision-making are formed during these years. By age five,

90 percent of a child's brain has developed. I was very aware of the importance of early development, and I worked hard to give Kevin every advantage. It wasn't easy. I tried to be everything to him, focused and attentive, but I struggled to make ends meet, to have time for my schoolwork, and to be everything Kevin deserved.

Feelings of self-doubt, insecurity, and low self-esteem had dominated my life, so I was definitely going to do things differently for my son. I wanted Kevin to have a strong sense of himself and a healthy self-esteem. I wanted Kevin to feel loved and valued. I wanted Kevin to have healthy relationships. So, I planned my life around connection and attention for my preschooler. Growing up in a large family had many positives like built-in friends with my brothers and sisters, always someone to play with, always something exciting going on. But, honestly, having that many children makes it hard to give each child the love and attention they need. I vowed to give Kevin the upbringing I didn't have.

I thought all I had learned through my education would help me shape Kevin's life. I could teach him about feelings and how to express them. I could model communication skills, educate him on how to be assertive rather than aggressive. While I was earning my master's, I took a class about substance abuse and addiction; learning about alcoholism and drug addiction was life-changing for me. I was very cognizant of the fact that Kevin had alcoholism on both sides of his genetic pool, and that worried me. I was terrified that Kevin would develop the disease of addiction, and I was determined to do everything in my power to prevent him from becoming an alcoholic or addict. Because of my training, I believed I could teach Kevin about the signs and dangers of addiction, which would protect him from the disease. Knowledge would "control" the genetic draw toward addiction, I falsely believed.

Kevin was full of life and had an astute ability to see beyond what was on the surface, which would often surprise me. I remember sitting on my bed one day when he was five. I was swirling in thoughts of overwhelm and frustration caused by school, shortened finances, and car problems. I had no idea how I was going to handle it all. I wiped a tear away when I heard Kevin come in and watched as he stood at the end of the bed, resting his arms on the mattress, placing his little face in his hands.

"What are you feeling?" he asked, with an empathy beyond his years.

I smiled. A therapist's son. *Maybe I am doing better than I thought,* I pondered with a smile.

Raising children is always a worry, even more so as a single parent, and I would often be concerned he did have only one parent. But when Kevin was thirteen, his biological father reached out to him for the first time. The reunion, however, was difficult, and Kevin wanted nothing more to do with him. He and I went to therapy after he met up with his dad, and the therapist was understanding and compassionate toward Kevin. He focused on the bond we had together instead of what Kevin was missing with his absent father.

The unbreakable bond.

"You've always been there for Kevin," the therapist said, reinforcing the idea that Kevin had never been abandoned, that I was showing up for him, that other people were showing up for him. My mom and dad were like second parents to him, my siblings were some of his best friends. Looking back, I think meeting his biological father helped him a lot because it enabled him to let go of the fantasies he had been holding on to about his dad. He could finally make his peace with it.

I thought.

———

After two years of stress and excitement, incomprehensible ups and downs, I was ready to breathe a sigh of relief; it had all worked out: I graduated from Arizona State University in August 1983. Kevin was six years old, and I was twenty-seven. I was proud of myself for managing to complete my master's degree while raising my son on my own. I believed in the profession I was entering, and I had developed a set of skills to not only get a job and make a living for us, but to be a better person and a better parent. Looking back, I incorrectly believed my education gave me some sense of being in control. I wanted Kevin to have a secure base from which he could learn to navigate the world. I thought therapy could solve many problems. I carried the belief that I could prevent future problems by educating my son and teaching him life skills.

But as most parents know, this was false thinking. No matter how hard I worked, no matter how much training I got, I couldn't spare my son from the realities of life.

CHAPTER 4
Kevin's Brain Injury

Kevin had a problem with alcohol. It started in high school when he got drunk, got caught, and was put on probation. He and his friend, both fourteen at the time, had to go through a program, which he completed—and then he didn't drink again. That is, until college.

He'd start slowly, but inevitably, danger reared up.

I remember one New Year's Eve, he was driving home and spotted some orange cones around a ditch. In his inebriated state he started to weave around them trying to avoid hitting one, he explained to me later. It caused him to almost teeter into a ditch. When he finally got home—safely—his stepdad and I were really shaken up when we noticed one of the orange cones stuck under the front of his car. Kevin must have run into the cone, a cone set up to warn a driver about a dangerous road situation. As I studied the cone stuck under his fender, all I kept thinking was, *he could have died that day*.

Kevin would go through these periods of binge drinking, then dry spells. He'd start out drinking with his friends, have a few beers—no big deal, and then, all of a sudden, he'd tie one on and something terrible would happen. Like the New Year's Eve-cone incident, like when he almost went over a cliff.

This time, he was with a friend, they had both been drinking. Kevin's decisions were not any clearer than his friend's; one choosing to get in a car with a visibly drunk driver, the other, his friend, being the drunk driver. Only the guardrail saved them. Kevin sustained some injuries to his eyes and had to take a break from college for a few weeks. The nurse who treated him said he was lucky to be alive.

By March 2007, I feared the drinking pattern was starting to escalate. At this time, Kevin worked for his stepdad, John, at John's roofing company. Occasionally, he would come to work hungover—or still drunk—then have to go home. Sometimes, he wouldn't show up at all.

I would confront him in exasperation: "You can't do this, it's wrong."

We would talk about alcoholism, especially how he was genetically predisposed to the disease. It was on both sides of his family tree. I realized, as I watched his pattern play out, that binge drinking was almost more difficult to identify and treat than daily drinking. It was easy to justify drink management when you've gone months or years without a sip of alcohol. For Kevin, it gave him an illusion of control and allowed him to continue denying the disease aspect of alcoholism. But every time, he'd be contrite; he said he understood, and it wouldn't happen again.

And then he'd go out and party with his friends, again.

Right after high school graduation, Kevin moved in with us—he had decided to stay in Arizona to finish his last two years of high school after I got married and moved to California. John never had to raise Kevin, so they had a different relationship. Less father-son, more friends. John was given tickets to many professional sports games as a benefit of his work as a roofing contractor. Kevin and John attended numerous games together, even getting floor seats at basketball games close to the action. Attending all those sporting events together cemented their relationship.

Kevin loved being John's stepson. He loved the stability John provided for our family. After graduating college, Kevin struggled to get work. He had a degree in communications, which was not exactly a path to a specific career. John was an accomplished business owner and a good example to Kevin of how hard work and perseverance could lead to financial and personal success in life. I decided they needed to work together..

One night I sat them down in the family room and said directly to them both, "Kevin, you need a job, and John, you need an estimator. Kevin, you are going to start working for John on Monday." Not much was said, and for some reason, they listened.

Kevin's drinking, and his decision to leave work or not show up at all, continually put John in a very difficult position with his other employees and led to a discussion about sending Kevin to rehab in order to keep his job. We wanted to use the job as leverage for a confrontation to get Kevin the help he needed. John explained that he would have fired any other employee by this point and that he didn't like how giving Kevin special privileges looked to the other employees.

"Kevin, you keep putting us in a very difficult position," we would say over and over, and he would nod his head, acknowledging it. I felt stuck in the middle, and it was painful. I felt guilty for harboring resentment toward Kevin for his behavior. John felt resentful, too, for being put in such an awkward position. He had no obligation to provide employment to Kevin, but John, as his stepfather, was trying to give Kevin a leg up in life and model hard work and success. Yet, all the begging, cajoling, yelling, threatening, crying, and explaining did nothing to propel Kevin toward sobriety.

I could feel it all coming to a head.

I GOT UP

The Sunday before the accident, Kevin came over for a BBQ. He hadn't been drinking with us, but still—I had a bad feeling. I walked him to the door as he was leaving that night.

"Be careful, Kevin," I'd said. "Something bad is going to happen." He dismissed me, not wanting to look at how his drinking was spiraling out of control.

Four days later, Kevin and his friends walked from work over to a nearby bar to watch the Sacramento Kings, our local professional basketball team. They were playing that night and the game was being televised—Kevin was having a great time with his friends and the alcohol was flowing.

The next morning, Friday, March 9, 2007, I got the call every mother dreads.

To be a parent is to always have an underlying fear that something terrible could happen to your child but we learn we must feel the fear and let our children live anyway. We can't keep them locked in a room somewhere safe from all the bad in the world.

After watching the game, Kevin and his friends wandered back from the bar to the parking lot at work. They hung around on the back of Kevin's pickup truck—ironically, recognizing they were too drunk to drive home, they planned to sober up first. Kevin, so I learned in fragments and bits and pieces over the days to come, had tried to climb over the side of the pickup truck and somehow lost his balance. No one is sure why he wanted to do this, maybe he needed to get down to use the bathroom, but Kevin's two friends, who were sitting on the tailgate, did not really see what happened. One minute, they explained, Kevin was standing on the bedside of the pickup truck, and the next he wasn't there. It was obvious he'd fallen, but not obvious how.

The next thing they knew, Kevin was unconscious; given the fact that Kevin was six feet tall and the height of the truck was several feet, the fall had the equivalent impact of tumbling out of a two-story building. Yet there was no external bleeding when Kevin's friends inspected him, they noticed only a few scrapes, and that he stayed unconscious.

But they, too, were drunk. They had lost all common sense, and their lapse in alcohol-fueled judgment would have devastating repercussions for us all. Though they couldn't rouse Kevin, they chalked his condition up to simply being drunk and passing out. Instead of calling an ambulance, or taking him to the hospital right away, they drove him home. Even when he didn't stir, and they had to drag him into the house, they didn't seem to be aware of the consequences of their actions. Kevin was a big guy and he lifted weights; carrying him into the house was like carrying a 250-pound dead body, so they chose to drag him under his arms into his bedroom. Later, I saw the bruising on his skin from the force required to get him inside.

When they were leaving, they warned one of Kevin's roommates that if Kevin died, they would beat him up.

One of the hardest things for me as a mother was to try to understand what they had been thinking. Were they afraid of getting in trouble with their boss, Kevin's stepdad? It had been after work, so they were free to go out drinking if they wanted, but still, their actions looked like the fear of children desperate to cover up a misdeed, terrified of getting in trouble.

"We just thought he'd passed out." . . . It was the only answer I would ever get.

Kevin's roommate Nick thought the whole ordeal was odd. By the time their second roommate came home from a date, they could hear Kevin vomiting and squealing in a high-pitched cry.

I would learn later that they tried to call me at that point, but I did not hear my phone.

It's strange how life can be mundane—until it's not. The reason why I didn't get Nick's call was because I was not in the room with my phone that night. John and I were getting new bedroom furniture. We'd moved all our old furniture out of the bedroom, making it ready for the new delivery the next day. In fact, Kevin was supposed to come over and help us move the furniture, and when he hadn't shown up, I knew he was out drinking. My numerous phone calls to him went unanswered which left me fuming. As I moved our old dresser through the doorway, I made a plan to confront him the next day. I rehearsed telling him he had to pull himself together.

Because the house was in somewhat of a disarray, John and I slept in our guest room, leaving our phones in their normal charging places, far from us. Never, in my wildest nightmares did I think we would be getting emergency calls in the wee hours of the morning. I would later learn the sequence of events that occurred as I slept.

When Nick couldn't reach me, they called another friend, Jordan.

"For God's sake," he cried. "Call an ambulance!"

The ambulance arrived to find Kevin unconscious, lying in the blood he had been vomiting. They rushed him to the emergency room at the closest hospital. When he arrived, he became combative and had to be sedated. This was evidence to the doctor that something was going on inside Kevin's brain. Then his breathing stopped, and they had to quickly intubate him.

Kevin had been literally minutes from dying.

A scan of Kevin's brain confirmed what the doctor suspected, a bleed on the brain. Technically, it was called a left epidural hematoma. Translated, that indicated a collection of blood in the space between the outer membrane of the brain and the skull. It was a life-threatening brain injury requiring immediate intervention. Temporoparietal intraparenchymal contusion was also part of the diagnosis and indicated bleeding in a specific area of the brain, which was extremely dangerous, carrying a very high mortality rate. Because Kevin's skull was fractured, too, they had to remove his skull, evacuate the bleed, and replace the damaged skull with a metal plate.

I would hear later that the only person the hospital staff could get a hold of was my mother, Kevin's grandmother, in Arizona. She was the first to learn Kevin was in the hospital having brain surgery.

And like Nick and the hospital staff, my mother, too, could not get a hold of me. So, she called my daughter Kara, who was seven years younger than Kevin. My mother was worried about alarming Kara, who was pregnant, so she waited until around 6:00 a.m. when she finally passed the news to Kara, who then called me. By then it was morning; I was awake, and finally, finally, heard my phone.

"Mom," Kara was crying when I answered her call. "You have to call Sutter Roseville Hospital. It's Kevin."

My heart stopped. Kara didn't have any details, so I hung up the phone and immediately called the hospital, one known for being an excellent Level II Trauma Center for their treatment of advanced-level trauma with life-threatening issues.

"Your son is on life support," the irritated nurse replied to my question tersely. "You need to come in and talk to the doctor."

Over the years that Kevin suffered with his traumatic brain injury, over all the doctors' appointments and rehab and counseling, I would encounter a spectrum of empathetic medical professionals. This nurse was not one of those, and it shocked me. She had just relayed the life-changing message that my son could be dying, and she was irritated? My head was spinning.

Still, I remained remarkably calm. I called a friend, though, and looking back, I'm not sure why. I suspect I was desperate for prayers from all my friends. I quickly threw on some clothes and headed to the hospital. It was about thirty minutes from my house but seemed like one of the longest drives of my life.

For a moment, I panicked.

"I can't do this," I cried. I was talking to my brother Steve, who was also crying. "I don't think Kevin is going to make it."

Somewhere in this crazy situation, Kara relayed the information about the brain surgery. It was all a terrible game of telephone. From the hospital's first call to my mother, then my mother's call to my daughter, then my daughter to me. I'd learned nothing from the hospital directly, but somehow, the original details about the brain surgery finally filtered through my family members to me.

"Well, at least he didn't hurt anyone else," I said to Kara flatly. Today, I have no idea why I said that, because at that moment, I hadn't a clue what had happened, or if anyone else was involved. I would only hear about the truck and the fall and dragging an unconscious Kevin home in snippets and overheard conversations over the next few days. It turned out I was right, that he hadn't, as I had once feared, driven drunk, crashed, or hurt another person. I can only assume my initial reaction was simply because I was in shock. I truly believed, from the nurse's comment, that I was being called in to decide to take Kevin off life support.

Again, a strange calm came over me. I didn't react or cry hysterically as John and I walked into the hospital where we were quickly directed to the ICU. We waited in an empty, barren, colorless hallway for the doctor to come out to talk to us. The wait, the agony, the whole situation, left a hollow pain in my stomach, like I had been punched in the gut.

At one point, I turned to my husband. "Where do I bury him?" Kevin had roots in Arizona where he grew up, but now we lived in California.

Where do I bury him?

I hadn't yet been able to ask what happened. I didn't even know that first morning in the hospital who had been with Kevin. My focus was completely narrowed down to the next moment and the decisions I might be forced to make.

A young doctor, who looked to be about Kevin's age, walked out of the ICU and greeted us in the hallway. "He's going to live."

The weight of the world suddenly lifted off my body and I thought I might collapse from the relief of it all. The doctor explained to us what they had found—that Kevin had a bleed on the brain which had to be suctioned out, and his skull on the left side had been shattered so it had to be replaced with a plate. That was it. That was all he said before he walked away. Our conversation was brief.

It was all I could absorb in the moment. I didn't even ask any questions as he turned and walked away. In my shock, the thinking part of my brain had gone completely offline, and I only had access to my emotions. Complete despair and blood-curdling fear transformed into life-altering relief and jubilation.

Your son is on life support.

Where do I bury him?

He's going to live.

We had cycled from the worst news to the best news. Lowest-low to highest-high in an hour. I wasn't sure whether I was going to vomit, pass out, or do a victory cheer.

In a way, I was somewhat grateful the hospital had not been able to reach me that night. I honestly don't know how I would have survived sitting in the ER, waiting helplessly, desperately, to find out if my son would survive the night. Now, at least, we knew he would live. But, I had no idea, none, the impact of TBI and how Kevin's life would never, ever be the same again.

CHAPTER 5

Critical Care

In the hours that followed, as we waited to see Kevin, I realized I felt no guilt about missing the initial phone calls, not when I realized there would have been nothing for me to do but worry all night. As it was, I felt momentarily rested, a state that would become fleeting in the coming days when sleep would be elusive.

The nurses finally let us know we could see Kevin and informed us that he was still under anesthesia, so he was not awake after surgery.

We crept into his room, and my heart sank when I saw him lying on the bed with a huge bandage wrapped around his head. It was a sudden feeling of shock. In fact, the pain that struck the moment I saw him almost doubled me over as if I had been hit right in the gut. All I could do was stare at my poor son, lying absolutely still in that hospital bed, with tubes snaking out of his body. I was helpless. Powerless. Heartbroken.

Friends began to arrive. Maria, who I'd initially called, had alerted other friends, and they gathered outside the ICU to offer me support and prayers. Nancy, a dear friend who, coincidentally, had herself just experienced brain surgery five days earlier, joined the group. It was an empty feeling, entering the world of trauma, ICU doctors, nurses, life and death decisions. I was removed from any reality I could comprehend. I was overwhelmed, but the love and support of my friends kept me afloat. I felt embraced by their presence and prayers.

While I was in the ICU waiting room with my friends, a nurse came to ask me for help with Kevin. They had decided to take him off sedation to assess how he was doing. I followed her back through the heavy, locked doors from the ICU and down a long hallway. Even from a distance, I could already hear Kevin screaming.

"We hope your presence can calm him, so we can evaluate him post-surgery," she explained as we hurried our steps.

I could hear Kevin screaming, "Nick! Get the gun! They have a gun!"

My breath stuttered. Whatever had happened with the fall had left his brain sensing danger.

"Kevin," I got right in his face, trying to get him to hear me.

But he kept violently thrashing as one ICU nurse tried to hold him down. A second one joined her; a third had to help, too, while a fourth got a shot ready to sedate him. They had to lay across his body to hold him down. Horrified, I watched as Kevin's writhing body lifted all three nurses up several times before the fourth nurse could finally give him the sedative. Immediately, he collapsed onto the bed.

The whole scene was haunting.

Traumatizing.

All I could think about was how I could still lose Kevin and how terrified I was. A nurse, noticing my distress, tried to calm me, tried to help me stay focused.

"Do you know anyone who has had a brain injury?" she asked, soothingly.

"Yes," I responded, trying to draw deep breaths. "She died."

Her name was Charity. Almost a year and a half before Kevin's accident, a dear, sweet, young woman, a former employee of John's, had moved to Australia to get a master's degree. Charity returned to the States to visit family and friends after graduating and before starting a new job. Charity was beautiful, bright, and had a great future ahead of her, which included a new boyfriend. She stopped by John's office to say hello and leave a bottle of wine from Australia, but John wasn't there. Later, when we heard the news, John would regret that lost moment.

Shortly after she returned to Australia, Charity was hit by a car as she stepped off the curb to cross the street. Even though the car was only estimated to be going twenty-five miles an hour, the impact spun her around and she fell, hitting her head. Charity died at the scene, but they resuscitated her. She was kept alive until her parents could fly to Australia to say goodbye before they took her off life support. We were all devastated. My husband's company was small, and she'd been like family.

So yes, I knew of someone who'd had a brain injury. I knew, in my limited experience, brain injuries did not have good outcomes.

Of course, I had no idea of what was to come. I had no idea how much—and how little—time I'd have left with Kevin, and my fears were overwhelming me. Was I, like Charity's parents, just there to say goodbye?

The nurse who'd ask me about my experience with brain injuries quickly changed the topic.

"Focus on just this one minute in front of you," she suggested. "Just this one minute. Then the next. And the next. One minute at a time."

CHAPTER 6

Presence

So, I did. I took it one moment at a time as I sat, waiting, in the ICU. It was like being in a time warp. You just sit in a chair watching your loved one struggling to survive. Life becomes narrowed down to only being in the ICU, it's the ultimate practice of being present; no cell phones or televisions offering distractions. Since I had been asked to keep my cell phone off, I couldn't call family or friends with updates. Time seemed to dissipate and dissolve as my reality was an unreality. I could barely leave Kevin's side to go to the bathroom because I was fixated only on Kevin with all the tubes and monitors coming out of his body. He was my sole priority and focus as if he were a newborn again. I don't even remember eating.

Of course, John drove me to the hospital the morning we had been awakened to such terrible news, and he stayed with me most of the day. Danny, my son with John, initially came to the hospital, but Maria, my dear friend, took him home with her for the rest of the day. Kara and her husband Matt also came to the hospital, but there wasn't much for them to do, and visitors were limited in the ICU. It was just waiting and watching, and waiting.

I heard later that some friends were angry with me for not returning their calls; their reaction baffled me. They were angry I was ignoring them? I was angry my son was near death! I would witness this again years later after Kevin's death, how other people would get upset when I wasn't acting or reacting in a way that fit their expectations. I think that's one of the most valuable lessons in empathy I have learned throughout all this. Not everyone handles trauma and grief in the same way—it's not a prescription. Why do we, as a society, insist that they do? To make it easier for those around us, I've concluded. But with each passing minute in the ICU and as I walked through my grief journey, I came to understand that it wasn't my duty to appease others or make them feel comfortable.

I had enough trouble holding myself together.

Later that afternoon, I began to put the pieces together of what happened to Kevin. The two young men who were partying with Kevin that night stopped by the hospital. One of them cried hysterically when he saw Kevin. The other one was stoic.

"What happened?" an ICU nurse asked them after the crying one had settled down.

"We thought he'd passed out from drinking. We thought we were doing the right thing by taking him home and putting him to bed." Shame filled their voices as they looked for somewhere else to direct their eyes.

"You never make a medical decision," the nurse berated them. "Always call an ambulance if somebody is down."

As she left, our friend Geoff, who was there with us, tried to comfort the two young men. "That's what we guys do, right? We watch a game and drink, and sometimes we drink too much."

While I appreciated Geoff's kindness, my own feelings were raw, complicated, and complex. I did feel sorry for Kevin's friends: I knew they meant no harm, that they made a very, very poor judgment call because of intoxication, not malice. Still, though, shouldn't we be held responsible for our actions, even while drunk—ESPECIALLY while drunk? If you drink and drive and get into an accident and kill someone, you're accountable. Wasn't this similar? What haunted me more, though, was that if Kevin had been taken to the ER sooner, he would have had less brain damage. His life would have been extraordinarily different if he had just gotten help. But ultimately, these thoughts were too much to bear, considering the outcome, and how it could have been so different. I had to shut away the what-ifs and if onlys so I could make space to concentrate on the here and now. I had to survive.

One minute at a time.

––––––––––––––––

Later that first day, the ER doctor returning for his evening shift stopped by, the one who saved Kevin's life by quickly assessing the situation and calling the trauma surgeon in to operate immediately. He came in, and though I was there, he said nothing to me, not even hello, or how are you doing. He simply stood there by Kevin, who was still sedated, watching him. I was far from offended; instead, I found it beautiful and caring. In fact, I didn't talk either. I couldn't speak. Sometimes there are moments when the only appropriate response is silence. It's sacred.

I never saw him again.

I did not get a chance to meet the trauma surgeon to thank him for saving Kevin's life that night either. He had been flown in from out of town in the middle of the night, and by the time we arrived in the morning, he was already gone. Like Superman, he came to save the day. Then, he was off again. Like a true hero.

By nightfall, the nurses advised me to go home and rest, reassuring me they would call if anything changed. I didn't feel I could be far from Kevin, though. Our house was a good half an hour away; it felt too far. I had to be closer, so we got a room at a hotel near the entrance to the hospital. I didn't even care that we had to sleep in our clothes. By six the next morning, I was up and back in the ICU, back to Kevin. I'd barely slept.

Doctors and nurses in the ICU have their own coping mechanisms. When I walked into the hospital the next day, Kevin's current doctor wouldn't make eye contact with me. I knew something was wrong.

The doctor addressed me cautiously. "Kevin isn't responding the way we hoped. He hasn't woken up on his own."

It must be so hard to tell a family their loved one might not make it. This doctor seemed to deal with it by not looking at me at all. I have learned when you are in a trauma like that, you need contact. But the doctor didn't want to connect.

I wept all day. And in those moments, I learned the difference between crying and weeping. Hard crying comes when you think you still have control of the outcome. Maybe if you cry hard enough or cry angry enough you can change the situation. Weeping comes from the realization that there is nothing you can do. It's a resignation. No amount of protesting with your tears will alter what is happening. Fortunately, the ICU nurses were compassionate, caring, and knowledgeable. They continued to reassure me Kevin would wake up. The day before, he'd occasionally tried to take off the restraints even though he'd remained heavily sedated.

"He must simply be exhausted from fighting to get up yesterday," one of them said. I was grateful for their encouragement, but I also knew that by day two, Kevin should have been more awake and alert. It was another blow.

We weren't giving up on Kevin, though. His whole family was there, taking turns to stay with him. John, of course, and Danny, though he was only ten, and Kara, and Matt.

We weren't going anywhere.

When I walked in the next day, I received a very different greeting. The doctor was smiling. He could look right at me. Eye-to-eye contact. "He's doing better. He's alert."

Thank God.

I was on a roller coaster of emotions. Highs and lows at dizzying speeds. From the first moment when the irritated nurse told me Kevin was on life support to news that he'd survived the surgery, then again through his thrashing and sedation, his inability to improve, and finally, his newfound alertness, I was up and down, happy and sad, relieved and despairing, and I could barely think straight.

It should have been a hint that my ride was far from over, but innocently, I believed the doctor's shining smile and our eye contact meant good news. It did, it was good news. But only in context from the terrible news of the day before. Because, when we walked in to see Kevin, he didn't recognize us. He couldn't say our names.

As his mother, I was crushed.

"Who am I?" we each asked. Me, his mother. John, his stepfather. Danny, his brother. Kara, his sister. Matt, his brother-in-law.

Who am I?

Kevin just stared blankly at all of our faces.

The experience was odd, and surreal in a way I'd never expected to experience, at least not from my child. How could Kevin, my son, not know who I was? We'd been a team, from the beginning. We shared a bond, tight and loving. It had been just the two of us for so long, and even as we added to our family, Kevin and I remained close.

Who am I?

The extent of Kevin's brain damage had yet to be determined. There was nothing we could do but wait and see.

CHAPTER 7

Waking Up

It was exhausting. Physically, emotionally, mentally. I was the one who stayed most often with Kevin. John would visit, giving me a chance to go home and take a shower, plus a much-needed break.

That was when the breakthrough happened. John told me later that he'd been sitting quietly—no surprise; John is a quiet man—when Kevin turned to look at him. "John, can you get me some water?"

He'd recognized John!

Kevin finally communicated, we deduced, out of a survival instinct. We'd been told that a person with a brain injury or someone who's had brain surgery must limit their water intake. It keeps the patient dehydrated to prevent their brain from swelling. As a precaution, he was only allowed ice chips, but Kevin had become so thirsty, he finally had to speak. It meant, at last, there was some hope.

Yet, it was hard to watch. He was nowhere near himself and was not enjoying being dehydrated. It was even harder not to give him a drink of water. You want to care for someone so fragile, but caring—in the way you think you should—could actually lead to life-threatening consequences. If we gave him the water, his brain could swell requiring more surgery and possibly more brain damage, even death. All I could do was offer occasional ice chips. The nurses would come in to monitor Kevin or give medication—they all loved him.

"Sweetheart, could you get me a glass of water?" Kevin would say to the nurses. He was still out of it. You don't wake up from a traumatic brain injury fully functioning. It takes a long time for the brain to heal.

"Oh, I like him," one nurse replied. "Nobody calls me sweetheart anymore."

It was a rare moment of levity. It made the situation seem almost normal for a second.

Kevin still had wires and monitors all over his body and half of his head was shaved. He had a horseshoe scar on the left side of his head with twenty-five staples keeping his head sealed. He'd lost at least twenty pounds, and I'm sure most people would have thought him a monster. Kevin was so weak and frail, like an innocent baby. It reawakened all my primal instincts to do anything to protect my child; I wanted to do everything I could to help him recover. It became my singular goal, taking tiny incremental steps forward.

Only in hindsight, though, can you appreciate just where those steps are leading you. If I had known just how rocky that path ahead would be, I think I would have wept in despair, teetering on hopelessness, perhaps I would have stopped. I didn't know much about brain injuries before all this happened—why would I? I would find that it became normal, how little information we would get from doctors. Most of what I learned, I had to learn on my own. In a world where information and education are keys to success, I was fortunate that I had access and the ability to keep digging, keep learning, keep pursuing any, and all, answers to help Kevin recover and adjust to his limitations—limitations we were wholly unaware of during those first few days in the ICU. But the more I fought, the more I advocated for my son, the more I also despaired. If I was struggling—and I was educated and experienced as a social worker—how did other people navigate the twisting minefields of traumatic brain injuries?

As Kevin slowly began to recover, I fell into a rhythm with taking care of Danny and attending to Kevin. Fortunately, I didn't work outside the home. When Danny started school, we realized he could benefit from additional, one-on-one support at home, so I put aside my professional life to focus on my family. When Kevin was in the hospital, I had the flexibility to be with him. That meant ensuring Danny was taken care of, too, and I was blessed with friends who came forward in different ways, from sharing a moment of pain and comfort with me, to offering me food, to picking up Danny from school.

I remember one day, about halfway through Kevin's third day in the ICU, that a friend showed up with a sandwich. We went outside, and I simply devoured it. As I licked the mustard off my finger, I realized I'd hardly eaten in the three days we had taken up post at Kevin's bedside. Just that one small, gracious, beautiful act of kindness alone, helped guide me through the darkness. As we sat on the bench outside the hospital, I suddenly realized I was alive as I registered the sun on my skin and filled my lungs with fresh air; I had a moment of respite. Life changes in the blink of an eye. I knew that in theory, we all do. But in that moment, I learned what it meant to hold space for the *and*; I was unlucky this had happened to my son, AND I was also extremely lucky to be blessed with amazing, loving friends.

Only, they couldn't be there for me all the time. I needed even more help, and I had expected my large, extended family to step up. I was collapsing under the stress. I was exhausting myself caring for Kevin, but also trying to be an attentive mother to Danny. I needed more support. I needed my family. I remember a meltdown one afternoon around the third or fourth day when I called my mother, my sister Mimi, and my brother John, all of whom lived in different states.

I GOT UP

"Where the fuck is my family?" I cried on the phone to my mother, then my sister, then my brother.

I got that they weren't local, but it pained me that as soon as my family heard Kevin would live, they all disappeared back into their own lives. For me and my immediate family, it turned out to be only the beginning of a very long nightmare. He was alive, but we couldn't know that living would take on a different meaning.

CHAPTER 8
Transitioning

It was day five in the ICU and Kevin was about to be discharged to the acute rehab facility. His doctor and a nurse came into the room and asked for a private moment. Not knowing what they were going to say, I felt cold dread wash over me. After finding a seat in a private consultation room, the doctor looked me squarely in the eye and wanted to know if the fall was a result of binge drinking. I felt tears sting the back of my throat as I shrugged my shoulders in answer; I didn't know the answer. I gave the doctor all the information I could about Kevin's history of drinking, but still, it seemed so unlikely that Kevin, who was an athlete, would lose his balance so tragically, even in the dark, even if he was drunk. The doctor never explained his reason for the question, but I wondered if the bleed on the brain was caused by a blood vessel that burst from alcohol. How had Kevin fallen from losing his footing in the dark? The thought that he had been drinking at the time of his accident was deeply disturbing to me. It's a mother's worst nightmare, that their child might be caught up in a life-changing catastrophe; now here we were in the middle of hell. I don't know with any certainty that his drinking that night contributed directly to his fall, but it couldn't have helped. I had worked in drug/alcohol treatment in my career; I knew the dangers, along with the challenges. It was hard to reconcile that, despite my experience in alcohol rehabilitation, I hadn't been able to help my own son. I had hoped to protect Kevin from the disease of alcoholism—but that's an illusion, believing you can control someone's genetic makeup. It is a cunning, baffling, and powerful disease, leaving everyone who faces it powerless in its grip.

The mother of Kevin's roommate, Nick, came to sit with Kevin for a few hours. I confessed to her that Kevin's drinking may have been a factor in his fall. I felt like I was burying myself under the weight of guilt I carried by not helping Kevin more. The idea that I didn't stop him just wouldn't let up. She looked at me with the empathy I profoundly needed to make it through the next minute, hour, day, and said simply, "Nobody deserves this."

It helped to be reminded of that fact, especially when it came from someone else. Whether alcohol did or did not play a factor in Kevin's fall was irrelevant; no one deserved the hand he had been dealt. It would be a tough road ahead—we could not have known how unpredictable and off-balance and chaotic our lives were about to become—but no matter what Kevin had or hadn't done, my big-hearted, smart, intelligent son did not deserve to have his life shattered like this.

What we couldn't appreciate then was just what those pieces of Kevin's life—and ours—would come to look like. We knew only what the doctor told us before Kevin went to rehab: that he would be alright but would have deficits. I had no idea what that meant, nor did the doctor offer any explanation, but I clung to the first part of the statement. He's going to be alright. I felt so relieved that I couldn't make room for anything else. That was what I'd been hoping and praying for all along. We all had.

He's going to be alright.

Every moment I studied his face looking for clues as to what the future held for him. My fantasy was that Kevin would go to rehab, rehabilitate his brain for three weeks, and then be back to normal. His head injury would be fixed—meaning everything was going to be okay. And after a few days, it wasn't just a fantasy—I strongly believed it. The doctor considered Kevin's age and felt he had youth on his side, which would help his brain to heal. The cut-off was thirty. Kevin was twenty-nine—phew. We barely made it. Kevin was lucky. I was so naïve.

I had no idea what was coming next.

The contrast of the ICU to rehab was startling. The doctors and nurses at the ICU had been the best of the best. They were knowledgeable and caring, especially the nurses. Their excellency had kept me focused and managed to keep me from being reduced to a heap on the floor. The ICU is a bubble; contact with the outside world is very limited, and so you become attached to them in your trauma, so much so, that it was almost hard to say goodbye. Thank you was an inadequate word to describe the gratitude I felt. After all, they had each played a part in saving Kevin's life.

CHAPTER 9

Rehab (for Brain Injury Survivors)

Leaving the cocoon of the ICU, padded from continuous care from the incredible doctors and nurses, and entering the acute rehabilitation facility at Mercy General Hospital was like being shot out of a cannon and landing in the middle of a desert. Hours passed in acute rehab before anybody even came in to talk to us. I watched staff walk by the door, seemingly ignoring us, as if we didn't exist. I finally approached the nurse's station in the center of the rehab unit, only to be blown off. In retrospect, this should have been a warning of things to come over the next three weeks. The facility cared for people with all different types of injuries, not just brain injuries, but it did not seem overcrowded, so I wasn't clear as to why we were being ignored. My trepidation grew as our wait stretched on and on. There was an unpredictability in not knowing what was going on that would become our new normal going forward.

Eventually, someone came in to do an assessment of Kevin, but in that moment, Kevin seemed so disoriented. I was filled with compassion for my son. If I was having trouble adjusting to the new situation, what was it like for Kevin? I could tell he was confused and didn't know what was happening to him. I was determined, therefore, to stay with him as a way to calm his anxiety and give him a sense of connection to someone who cared. It did seem to help him.

Over the next few days, Kevin's physical abilities were assessed. He did not have any issues related to coordination and could still dribble a basketball. As I listened to the thud of the ball hitting the tile floor, I let out a sigh of relief. Sports were such an integral part of Kevin—it would have killed both of us to watch that ability slip away. However, my relief was short-lived.

The results of the psychological evaluation proved not to be overly promising as we realized Kevin was having trouble recalling words. The psychologist gave him notecards with words on them to practice. Simple words. Words you would use in teaching little children to read. *Ball* or *car* would get Kevin so frustrated as he tried to will his damaged brain to recall the words he had learned in kindergarten. The frustration would cause extreme agitation and overload, so the psychologist would stop. She left the words with me to practice with him, but as he tried to read the words again, he would go from frustrated to angry. Watching him struggle broke my heart. The four-year-old wonder boy who was reading in preschool, now as a grown man couldn't recall the word *toy*. It gutted me, and I was scared because no one would say it would get better or how much better it would get. The medical professionals weren't psychic; they had no crystal ball to tell us how Kevin's recovery would progress, and I knew that, but still, as I watched him struggle with his word recall, I carried the weight of not knowing for him.

"Just keep working with him," they would say.

One morning an attractive female psychologist came by to do an assessment. My heart sank as I watched Kevin get up in the middle of the assessment, walk to the toilet, unzip his pants, and relieve himself in full view of me and the psychologist.

"He's lost social cues," the psychologist explained quietly, as my eyes looked for something else to focus on other than my adult son peeing six feet away from me.

I had been so focused on his word recall that I had never considered the social side of things. My eyes filled with tears as I realized we had to deal with yet another loss from the brain injury.

"Will this improve?" I asked her. And my question hung in the air between us. Would Kevin regain his social intuition? He was a very gregarious guy. He would have never urinated in front of anyone before. It was a new area to work on and worry about. How was Kevin going to manage? And this underlying thought, while embarrassing to admit: how was I going to manage?

One evening, after returning from picking up Danny at school and grabbing some pizza to take to Kevin at the hospital, I walked into the rehab to find Kevin zipped up in a mesh tent which covered his bed. He was standing upright. The tent was zipped up from the outside so he could not get out, but he was trying. I wanted to scream out in pain. I still do, even years later. Kevin reminded me of an animal in a cage. Trapped. Restless. Scared.

"This is what we do for a patient when they start to come to after a head injury, to protect them," the staff said, explaining the specialized enclosure bed encapsulating my son.

Protect them from what? I wondered.

As I watched him continue to struggle from the inside of the mesh tent, I thought I was going to throw up.

I did my best to calm Kevin, but he was terrified and unhappy, and I couldn't blame him.

Sometime the next day, while waiting for Kevin to finish rehab therapy, I was approached by a staff member. "You should go home," she told me. "It isn't necessary for you to be at the hospital all the time."

I stared at her for an entire minute. *Then why is my intuition telling me differently?* I wondered. I was not interfering with any of his treatment, and I knew in my gut that Kevin did better with me being by his side; I was a calming influence on him. Dismissing my gut instinct had always rendered bad decisions in my life, but for some reason, I listened to her, despite my misgivings, and decided to stay home the next day. There, as I sat sipping coffee, I worried the whole time about Kevin, but tried to reassure myself that he'd be fine. I looked around, reminded that I did have to focus on other parts of my life. Still, I was anxious.

Then I got a call from the hospital.

"Is Kevin with you? Do you know where he is?" the nurse asked from the other end of the line.

"No . . ." I answered in confusion.

He'd left the hospital.

What the fuck?

"You told me not to come in the other day when I was at the hospital!" I cried. "You promised he'd be fine!"

How could this be happening? How could they lose my son? I was panic-stricken.

The staff had no idea where he was or how long he had been gone. John and I jumped in the car and drove the forty-five minutes to Sacramento to begin searching for him. It was on us to find him; the hospital had not even called the police, and they never explained why they didn't contact the police to begin a search for him.

"This is what brain injured people do," they explained with a shrug.

My mind jumped to worst-case scenarios, but immediately, I fled from those thoughts. I couldn't go there. I'd just gotten Kevin back from the brink of death; I couldn't let myself consider him being gone for good.

We stopped by his regular haircut spot. No one had seen him. Frantic, we drove all around the housing area and shops within walking distance of the hospital. What was even more mystifying was that Kevin had walked out of rehab wearing an ankle monitor that was supposed to beep when he left the premises, but no one had heard it because they were desensitized to the sound. Every time the door opened and shut, it was accompanied by a BEEEPPP. I'd noticed it every time, and now I was furious—what was the point of having a safety system in place if it was just ignored?

There was no doubt Kevin was extraordinarily vulnerable. He may have been a big guy, but he had half his head shaved, and twenty-five staples exposed. He was wearing a hospital-grade top and drawstring pants designed with a slit for using the bathroom, but no underwear. Both items had the name of the hospital on them. When I realized he had left in his Air Jordan sneakers I remembered that people have been killed over Michael Jordan shoes. My heart raced and my need to find him became even more desperate.

Our impromptu search party quickly turned into organized chaos. My cousin Stephanie lived near the hospital, so I called on the off chance to see if Kevin had shown up at her house. He hadn't. She joined the search immediately, and I gushed with gratitude. She kept me calm that day—as calm as possible, anyway. She was focused and competent and soothing, and it was exactly what I needed. It's funny, even in some of our most desperate moments, God knows what we need and provides. After alerting Kara and Matt, together with some friends, they rushed to Sacramento to help us with our search. After a while, I realized we were too strung out. We had no home base, so I suggested Kara and Matt return to my house in case Kevin called.

When she got home, Kara realized that Kevin had called the house. She immediately got a hold of me.

"Mom, he did call," Kara said, and a wave of relief washed over me.

Thank God. He was alive.

"But he didn't leave a location or any other information."

The dread returned as quickly as it had left, but Kara kept talking. "We called back the number Kevin used—it was from a phone owned by a server at a restaurant in South Sacramento."

How the hell did he end up in South Sacramento? It was at least a half hour away driving. It must have taken him hours to walk there. It wasn't the best part of town; in fact, it was downright dangerous. My anxiety built as we drove to the area.

"I just thought he was mentally ill," the server explained when we located her.

I was seething. "So, you didn't notice the staples in his head? You didn't notice the hospital clothing?" Could she not see he was vulnerable? Could she not have done more to help him?

"Sorry," she said and walked away to attend to another table.

We went to a mobile phone store next to the restaurant to see if they knew anything. The young man working there said he had seen someone fitting Kevin's description.

"You better find him," he warned. "He walked right out into oncoming traffic."

"Oh my God," was all I could say in response. I looked out the window front and surveyed the scene. It was a very busy main thoroughfare. He was going to get killed walking out into traffic or, at the very least, robbed for his shoes. I tasted bile as the anxiety mounted in my chest. I could barely think.

As we paced up and down the side of the busy streets, cars zipping by, we agreed we needed more help. Since Matt and Kara were waiting at home, they easily contacted a local news station, requesting they air information about a missing person for the five o'clock news. The station was more than willing but needed a picture, which became problematic given that Kevin did not presently look like any of the pictures we had on hand.

Shoot. Why hadn't I taken a photo of him in rehab with my phone? Someone took pictures of him in the ICU but we didn't think to take a new picture in rehab. Not yet. I was busy berating myself as my eyes continued to scan the horizon. Searching for Kevin was more difficult than looking for a needle in a haystack. None of us knew where to look. If it had been "Before Kevin," then maybe we had a small chance of figuring out what he was thinking, but with this brain injury, well, he was entirely unpredictable. We drove around the area where he had last been seen, but to no avail. None of us could figure out what led him to South Sacramento. What could he possibly have been thinking?

Please God, I begged. *Please watch over him. Mother Mary, please help Kevin. Please. He's so incapable right now of knowing what he is fully doing. He's like a child.*

When we went into a hotel near the restaurant just out of desperation, we learned even worse news. They said he had come in and now a man was seen following him. The hotel clerk did not think the man was someone to be trusted.

Oh my God. He was in danger. Terror flooded my veins. I was nauseous. We were at an impasse; we didn't know where to look next, and I couldn't take it anymore.

Six hours had passed since our search began—my heart got heavier as we realized it would soon be getting dark. I couldn't deal with the thoughts of Kevin not having a place to sleep that night when it was cold, or worse, getting beat up for his shoes. And more than those thoughts, I was terrified of losing him. We almost had once.

"It's Kara!" I shouted. *Finally!* I started praying it would be good news.

"Mom, Kevin called. He's talking gibberish, but I think I was able to make out he is at the Embassy Suites in Sacramento."

I GOT UP

John and I had split up to widen our search, and Stephanie and I were in her car. As soon as John got the news, he barreled toward an Embassy Suites hotel, located near the local baseball stadium, home to the River Cats, a Triple-A minor league team. Kevin had worked for the River Cats as an announcer so he was familiar with that area of Sacramento. But Kevin, in his confused state, had hung up on Kara before she could be sure. This location was another half an hour from where we were looking, in a completely different area of town.

Stephanie and I couldn't get there fast enough.

I called the hotel, asking if someone meeting Kevin's description was in the lobby. They had located him. "Please," I begged, "don't let him leave."

John arrived before us, and finally he called, panting. "I've got him. I've got him."

I almost collapsed from exhausted relief. We'd found Kevin. He was alive. He was unharmed. He was safe.

It had been the scariest day of our lives. Those six, terror-inducing hours were hell. An ordeal I wasn't sure we'd all survive.

And then, when we walked into the hotel lobby, Kevin greeted us with a smile and a nonchalant, "What have you guys been up to today?"

I almost passed out.

It was the brain injury. He had no clue. And I didn't know if I had the strength to take it.

CHAPTER 10

Lost and Found

The hotel staff, unaware that we were running all over Sacramento, had alerted the police, who showed up a short time later. I'm sure the whole thing sounded crazy to them, but after questioning us, they released Kevin back to our custody.

The last thing I wanted to do was return to the rehab facility. They'd been remiss in their duties, rendering Kevin missing—I was too furious for words. All I wanted to do was gather his things and take him home.

"He won't get the rehab he needs if you do," they told me.

The hospital staff showed no remorse. My body was shaking with rage, but I didn't know if it was their extreme negligence or the fact that I knew they were right. Kevin needed trained medical staff to care for him at this time—and that wasn't me. Reluctantly, I agreed to keep him there, but I was definitely going to stay with him. There was no way I was trusting the staff to keep an eye on him, not after their horrific negligence earlier. They pulled in a mattress for me to sleep on and placed it on the floor. The floor was filthy, and disgusting. I was wedged behind Kevin's bed and the wall behind him, and he called out to me several times that night to make sure I was with him.

"Kevin, I'm right here," I reassured him, weary in my bones.

It was weeks before we'd managed to piece together what had happened. Kevin didn't have clear memories of that day; they were jumbled and confused. He'd gone to the bank, he said, and, because—of all things—he remembered his PIN code, he was able to withdraw $200. There was a bus stop right outside the bank, and he got on, finally ending up in South Sacramento because of a store he knew where he could buy a particular video game. It was being released that day. He remembered the game release date and where he could purchase the game, yet when he got there, he became confused. That was when he'd walked into the restaurant and asked the server if he could use her phone, leaving us a message. And he had walked right into traffic. Cars whizzed past him; he almost walked out in front of a bus. Later, Kevin told me he didn't like to think about that day: "I can still feel the wind of that bus, it was so close to my face."

He had made it to the mall to buy his game but must have grown even more disoriented. For some reason, the security guard kicked him out of the mall when he tried to ask people for help. I was seething when I heard this. Instead of calling the police, or the hospital—whose name was stamped clearly on Kevin's clothes—the security guard had kicked him out. It is so disheartening to think how people treated him when he was so vulnerable.

I remember Kevin relaying a heartbreaking experience he'd had that afternoon: he asked a woman in the hotel shop, "Do I seem dumb to you? People are treating me like I'm dumb." If my heart could crack any more, it would have. No, Kevin was not dumb. Yes, he was acting differently. Odd. Unbalanced, even, but if anyone had taken even a minute to talk to him, they would have seen that no, Kevin was not dumb. Kevin, recovering from a traumatic brain injury, simply needed help. And it was only Kevin's resourcefulness that saved him. He was the one, despite his impairments, to try calling home, and calling home multiple times until we could find him.

Interestingly, he did get the video game.

As much as I wanted to stay with Kevin 24/7, I knew I couldn't. I had another son at home who also needed me, so the following evening, with the sworn oaths of the hospital staff to watch Kevin closely, I went home. I had insisted that Kevin get to keep his phone, though, in case he managed to escape again. At least that way we'd easily be able to locate him.

Later that night, Kevin's friend called me.

"Kevin called," he said. "He asked me to pick him up, and said he'd meet me outside the hospital."

Fear again flooded my veins. I was beyond grateful for the heads-up, and I immediately notified the staff. Could they not see how much of a flight risk Kevin still was? I believe they ended up zipping him into the tent that night, and it was no surprise to me that, when I arrived the next morning, he'd been moved to a different room. One closer to the nurse's station.

I had a meeting set up with a representative from the hospital.

"This is what brain-injured people do. They wake up, don't realize what happened, or where they are, so they leave."

I remember her saying it so casually, without any air of concern. Could she not appreciate what had almost happened to him? Is this what happened to all the brain-injured patients they treated? They just got up and walked out of the hospital and into oncoming traffic and everyone just accepted it? They had met the wrong mother.

"He's not just any patient to me!" I cried. "He is my son! He almost died. I'm not going to let him die on the street because he escaped the hospital and you couldn't find him."

She just blankly stared at me, provoking my anger to seething. She was blaming the patient. It was his fault he left the hospital. *This was my son!* He wasn't just a number, a patient. He was a living, breathing, vulnerable human being who had a family who loved him.

It didn't get better. Shortly after this conversation, another nurse sought me out.

"Kevin was found outside again," she told me in secret. "I just thought you should know."

I was shocked. After everything we'd been through, the staff hadn't even planned to let me know that they'd let him escape again. It was only pure luck that a staff member saw him outside the window and hurried to bring him back.

Honestly, I didn't think my heart could have taken another escape.

Since the acute rehab was part of a Catholic hospital, nuns would often work there, visiting patients. One of them had talked to Stephanie when Kevin went missing the first time. When she heard Kevin had escaped again, she came to speak with me.

"Go across the street to the administrative offices," she told me. She suggested I ask to speak to a particular woman who oversaw the hospital. "Tell them you'll wait for her."

So, I did. I informed them the Sister had sent me over, and that I would wait. Finally, the executive called me in and listened but she, too, downplayed the situation.

"This is what brain injured people do."

What kind of answer was that? It was on repeat from almost everyone I encountered at the hospital.

I needed another tactic. I searched through the exhausted spaces in my mind for what to say and a lightbulb went off.

"Listen, because of your lack of support during our search for Kevin, we were forced to contact a local news station to do a story on Kevin's escape. They were waiting for Kevin's picture when we found him. They were planning to air the story."

Her head snapped up from the file she had been perusing as a silent gesture for me to leave.

Well now, *that* got her attention.

"You mean they were going to put it on the news?" Her jaw dropped in disbelief.

"Yes," I emphasized again. "They were just waiting for a picture."

She called over the man in charge of the rehab unit, and he changed his tune. Real quick. I had to shake my head. My concerns as a mother and family member weren't enough. Kevin's care and well-being weren't enough. Only the fear of exposure forced them to act. Their concern for their reputation as the priority made them decide to hire a nurse to sit outside the door to his room to make sure he didn't leave.

I was relieved, but so, so tired. Every part of me was depleted. Not just because of Kevin, but from fighting with the system. Why did I have to fight for the care and protection my son needed? And what happens to people who don't have the skills I have as a social worker to confront this situation? Or who are too intimidated to speak? Or too scared? Or don't speak the language? I didn't realize it then, but it was only the beginning of my fight to get him the care he needed.

This entire situation, from the escape from rehab to the return to the hospital, woke me up to the reality of how disabled people are treated in our society; as less than, as ignored and devalued. From the server in the restaurant to the security guard in the mall, to the staff at the acute rehab facility, I witnessed how people view a person with a disability or mental illness. I became aware. Now I can't unsee it. It was devastating to see my son become permanently disabled and also become rejected by society. Where is our compassion? Where is our concern for helping others in need? How do we so easily reject others who are different from us? It's a painful awakening.

In the end, I'm not convinced rehab even helped. I could have done so many of the exercises they gave him to do at home with direction, a little training, and support. All of that effort, all of the fear and terror of Kevin being missing, all of the stress to calm him, and it was not the outcome, in the end, we had hoped to see.

CHAPTER 11

Running on Empty

They always tell you when you get on an airplane that you should grab your oxygen mask first before you help someone else. It sounds reasonable, of course, but no one tells you that there are situations in life where the oxygen mask simply just doesn't exist. Women are used to this, but as a mother in a situation like ours, it took on a whole other meaning. I functioned for Kevin's sake, Danny's sake, even John's sake, but it cost me my own. No one seemed to notice that I was running out of air.

Though, to be fair, once I'd asked my mother and sister to come for five days, I got a short breather. Mimi helped Danny with homework and driving to school, and both she and my mother were calming influences on the household, which then allowed me to focus most of my energy on Kevin. They saw how hard it was for me because I simply had no help.

"Why is he not driving you to the hospital?" my mother asked me one morning, feeling frustrated as she watched John walk out the door.

The truth, I felt, was John didn't want to fully face what was happening to Kevin. It made him too sad. After Kevin left the ICU,

John returned his focus to running his business. I realized that I had shot myself in the foot when I had spent our entire marriage taking care of everything. John saw me as competent and capable. I didn't ask for much. But I had never needed much either. Until now.

I'm not sure how I managed to do it all. The stress was so bad it would cause me to physically shake. As the second oldest of ten children, I had learned early in my life to jump in and do whatever needed to be done. I was taught to push my feelings aside and take care of the little kids. From childhood to adulthood I was used to doing it all—and it had become our way between me and my husband. After I told him what my mother said, John drove me to the hospital that night, but I still felt alone in the primary care for Kevin.

I wanted to believe Kevin was going to be fixed. If I stayed in control, everything would work out, which equated to creating a reality where Kevin could return to "normal." I desperately wanted to believe the head injury could heal over time. Even though I was beginning to realize life had changed dramatically for not just Kevin but for all of us, I held onto hope. Every time Kevin remembered a word, I was encouraged. I felt like a proud mother of a kindergartner learning to read for the first time.

Kevin became very talkative in rehab, more than usual. His conversations were intense, philosophical at times, reflecting on certain areas of his life but without any real awareness of what happened to him. He didn't talk about the accident. He couldn't remember it. He had no idea what had happened to him.

"Mom, I was a really good basketball player in high school. It was my dream to play college basketball. I should have moved here in high school. But, Winslow was a good place for me to be."

"I hope someday to take over John's company. Jim came by with a basketball signed by all the guys at work." Jim was John's business partner.

I just listened mostly.

"Yeah, you were a good basketball player."

"Yeah, maybe someday, you'll take over the company." It would be a year and a half before he would even return to work.

Kevin was still the same with the same interests and concerns, but also desperately trying to piece his mind back together again. It was as if his brain knew it had been hurt and was in hypermode trying to get back to normal again.

There was so much we didn't know or understand.

The medical staff did not provide adequate information on traumatic brain injuries to me. Their job is to treat the patient. But, I could have used education. I could have used a social worker to sit with me and hand me a packet explaining TBIs. All they told me was he would have deficits. As a social worker myself, I am an avid researcher and very capable when it comes to identifying resources. However, I was stuck in the hospital for hours with no access to a computer or internet service. When I got home at night, I took care of my younger son before collapsing in bed from exhaustion. Research would have to wait. We were in survival mode.

Thankfully a girlfriend who was a speech pathologist dropped by weeks later with a packet of information on traumatic brain injury. With this information and time to research I would later learn that everyone who has TBI will have unique symptoms depending on the area of the brain that was damaged. However, some things are true for almost everyone with TBI such as difficulty sleeping, difficulty regulating emotions, difficulty multitasking, short-term memory loss, and difficulty processing. I had no idea what any of that would look like in the future.

Mostly, Kevin and I had to learn the hard way. We learned it by living it. It was the most comprehensive, stressful, chaotic, unpredictable on-the-job-training I'd ever had.

CHAPTER 12

Homecoming

After five days in the ICU and three weeks in acute rehabilitation, Kevin was finally coming home. I was ecstatic that he would be released from medical care for many reasons, but his liberation was mine too. No more long drives back and forth, and no more long days spent at the acute rehab facility.

Prior to discharge, the doctor's last words to me were ominous and filled with warning: "If you have a job, quit it. From this moment on, Kevin will need full time care."

I was shocked. *Quit my job?*

Of the month we had been in the hospital, not one nurse or doctor had mentioned Kevin would require so much care.

Kevin was happy to come home. We were all excited but none of us understood yet what it meant to have a brain injury and just how dramatically our lives would change.

The first thing Kevin asked for was a haircut. I stared warily at the horseshoe shaped scar on the side of his head. About to challenge his request, I remembered Kevin loved his visits to his barbershop in Sacramento. He was a regular, with weekly visits to keep his hair looking good; and he also wanted to interact with the other guys at the barbershop because they loved shooting the shit about sports. I waited in the car, basking in the glow of thinking it was a normal thing for him to want to do. It was a good sign, and God knew I was ready for one. If this one thing was alright, surely, it meant everything else would be too.

As Kevin walked back to the car, I could see he felt right in himself again. His hair was just how he liked it, scar and all.

The next morning Kevin woke up, walking slowly from his bedroom, he came over, and sat on the couch.

Looking confused and a little lost, he asked me, "Mom, what do you do when you get up in the morning?"

I was stunned.

"What do you mean?" I asked nervously. "You . . . get up. Get ready."

Keving looked at me blankly and as I surveyed the remnants of his broken skull, it took me little time to realize things were not better. Kevin didn't know how to do basic, daily tasks like brushing his teeth, having a cup of coffee, or planning for the day ahead. We had to break down the morning routine into simple steps. Wake up. Go to the bathroom. Drink a cup of coffee. Eat breakfast. Shower. Brush your teeth. He needed each action to be broken down into singular specific steps. Even something as simple as taking a shower became complicated for him. Kevin would spend nearly an hour under the water, because he would forget what part of his body he had already washed, and have to start again.

It scared him, and it scared me. How could he not remember how to get ready in the morning, but he could remember his PIN code for the bank? How could he be okay with the guys at the barbershop but forget how to shower?

Together, we developed a plan for every step. We plotted a strategy for his shower: start with your head and work your way down the body. And if you forget, that's okay; no harm in washing twice, or missing a body part altogether. Because of his short-term memory loss, Kevin had to relearn the simple, ordinary tasks people do every day without thinking. He had to practice until they became routine again. In our brainstorming, I suggested he take a video of some of the tasks so he could replay it if he got stuck. His iPhone, therefore, became an extension of his brain, and helped him recover a sense of independence most of us simply take for granted. Kevin did eventually develop the basic skills for daily living, but his short-term memory never fully recovered. He made incredible progress which was so encouraging. *Neuroplasticity* they call it. Watching how the brain can develop new pathways was truly remarkable. And while his brain never fully healed from the traumatic injury, Kevin was eventually able to function on his own again.

My fantasy that life would get easier with Kevin's return home was short-lived. I had to drive him to outpatient rehabilitation at least three days a week. I also had to drive him to doctors' appointments. And I was dropping Danny off at school, and picking him up after school, and taking him to any extracurricular activities. Kevin's outpatient rehab and the doctor's offices were at least forty-five minutes away from our house in the opposite direction of Danny's school. The outpatient rehab was an hour from Danny's school. Since Kevin's license had been suspended for six months because of his brain injury, and there was no Lyft or Uber services at the time, all the driving was left up to me. Every day, I spent hours in the car. It was nothing to spend four-to-five hours taking my kids where they needed to go.

And then, I understood why the doctor told me to quit my job.

And all of this—it was killing me. My insides were shaking; my stamina for taking care of everyone else was plummeting, but I knew without a doubt, I had to remain calm on the outside. Instinctively, I knew my nervous system needed to coregulate Kevin's and Danny's nervous systems, or it would have been crazy. I had to appear calm, stable, and hopeful. I was the mom. Was it the grace of God that got me through that time? Just perseverance? I found myself often recalling the advice from the ICU nurse: "Focus one minute at a time."

I had gotten through the minutes, and now it was days, but I could only focus on the here and now, could now only focus one day at a time, one task at a time. *Do what is immediately in front of you. Don't focus on even the next thing.* It was all I could do to survive. There was no fixing it. There was no one to rescue me.

And I failed, of course I did. No one can be everything to everyone, so, in retrospect, I recognize it wasn't failure, that I did the best I could at the time, but no matter my actions, there were always consequences. How Danny got left behind was one significant one.

Danny gained a lot of weight during that time, and, in a way reserved solely for mothers, I blamed myself. His school did not have a school lunch program, so I bought lunch from the deli next door. They would deliver a huge sandwich, chips, a drink, and a cookie. It was not a child-sized lunch, and he was only ten. Under normal circumstances, I would never have provided lunch like that for a child, but honestly, I had no energy to make lunches every day. I suspect his sister and dad were also offering him comfort foods. It was one way to make him feel better, because how was a ten-year-old child supposed to process what had happened to his big brother? There was a large age gap between them, nineteen years, but Danny loved Kevin. They had vastly different personalities, but they'd always been brothers. When Danny had visited Kevin in acute rehab, he gave Kevin such a big hug. Almost losing Kevin was too much for Danny to handle emotionally. He had no way to put his feelings to words or comprehend the changes he saw in Kevin. If none of the adults really appreciated what was happening to Kevin, how could Danny have understood?

It was yet another fallout of Kevin's accident. And more, so many more, impacts were still to come.

CHAPTER 13

Aftercare

Winston Churchill is credited for saying, "If you're going through hell, keep going." I remember reading that line a few years after this story all unfolded and it hit me right between the eyes. We were living in hell. I'm sure Churchill made this statement in reference to world wars, but I was fighting my own battle, and Kevin was right there in the trenches with me.

The medical approach to TBIs in the United States is to release patients from rehabilitation after reaching a certain level of care, and turn subsequent care over to family members. Upon Kevin's release from the rehab facility, the only thing that was clear was that it was going to be up to me to arrange ongoing medical care for Kevin. He would need a primary care doctor, a neurologist, and a host of other medical professionals to oversee his long recovery. Outpatient rehab would meet some of his needs, but certainly not all of them. But who was I to pick up where the medical team faded off? I was just a mom. Yes, I was a licensed clinical social worker, but I was not an expert on traumatic brain injury. I was being asked, no, required, to perform above and beyond my level of expertise. It was a daunting task, to say the least.

I started out in this new position by using the skills that I had always employed as a social worker. I started searching for the right healthcare professionals, ones I hoped would "fix" Kevin. In short, I wanted the best doctors we could find. Kevin's primary care doctor had been highly recommended by a friend who was a nurse. This primary care doctor then referred Kevin to a neurologist he thought highly of for ongoing care. This neurologist read the hospital report, looked right at Kevin, and said simply, "You are lucky to be alive."

I didn't know until we met with this doctor that Kevin had stopped breathing when he arrived at the ER the night of his accident. I knew he had become combative, which alerted the ER doctor to a possible injury to the brain. I also knew he had to be intubated, but with everything that had been going on, I hadn't processed the fact that intubation was a medical procedure used when a person isn't breathing on their own. How could I know that? I was not a medical professional, and was drowning in all the foreign words and medical information. When the ambulance picked Kevin up at his home, he was rushed to the ER, where he had stopped breathing soon after his arrival. Within minutes, he'd been intubated to save his life. We had an abstract knowledge that Kevin had almost died, but it was disturbing to hear from this doctor how close he'd been to death that night. If no one had called 911, and he had not been taken to the hospital right at that moment, Kevin surely would have died.

We were all shaken, but Kevin was especially rattled by this news.

He had no memory of the fall, only that he'd been with his friends, and then the next thing he remembered was waking up in the hospital.

The neurologist was kind but informed us that Kevin's TBI was not his area of expertise, so he sent us on our way. Kevin's primary care doctor sent another referral to a different neurologist. Referrals take time. Nobody was in a rush for us to get our questions answered or set up ongoing care. One thing I learned through this process is that doctors don't like to admit they don't know how to treat something. They want to provide answers, but TBIs are difficult to treat, and the reality is, there just aren't many answers.

The deficits to the brain are unclear in the beginning, so it's hard to predict how much recovery a person can achieve. In the twenty-first century, it is shocking to realize that the brain is a new frontier. Sadly, it is the soldiers coming back from Iraq and Afghanistan who paved the way for new and better ways to treat a brain injury, and while I applaud the efforts of the medical community to support and heal these individuals, I can't help but wonder about the rest of us.

The second neurologist we finally got in to see wasn't very sympathetic.

"Why are they sending you to me?" he asked curtly, looking at his watch, communicating we were wasting his time.

Maybe because you are supposed to know something about the brain? I wanted to answer. Instead, I stayed silent as Kevin and I exited his office in a cloud of hopelessness. We had so many unanswered questions. And nowhere to find the answers. What could we expect in Kevin's recovery? Would he be able to return to work? Were there any medications that would help? Any that would be harmful? We didn't know what to do next. We had nowhere to turn. We felt abandoned by the medical community as we were pawned off from one medical professional to the other. Yet, in the nightmare, Kevin and I had our bond.

It was a "we" thing, a team effort focused on getting Kevin better, so we did what we had always done. We simply put one foot in front of the other. Kevin always said we had a bond that could not be broken, and the brain injury seemed to weave us, fasten us, together in a way we hadn't been connected before. In some way, maybe the lack of information was a good thing. It kept us moving forward, searching for a different solution, just as we had from the very beginning. We just couldn't accept this was how it was going to be from now on. We had each other, as always, and we were going to triumph—why would it ever be anything different?

CHAPTER 14

Facing Reality

About a year after the accident, we decided a short trip to Seattle would be good for everyone. John, Danny, Kevin, and I loved going to Seattle, and would always stay at The Edgewater Hotel, situated on a pier over Elliott Bay, right on the water. Pike Place Market had the most beautiful fruit, my favorite was always the Oh My God peaches so accurately advertised because when one would sink their teeth into the yellow flesh, all you could do was moan, "Oh my God!" Yes, they were that good!

All weekend we strolled around the city, consuming fresh fish, and drinking way too much local coffee. Kevin's passion for sports was still alive and well, and time was set aside to go see the Seattle Mariners play baseball. Kevin was improving every day, and every day as I watched him get closer to himself, I breathed a sigh of relief. Until one night when we were having dinner at The Edgewater, my head snapped up to look straight at Kevin when he gave his order to the server with a new and strange accent. The way he pronounced the word "salmon" had a southwestern twang to it. And it was disturbing. This wasn't Kevin.

Out of a surprised reaction, I snapped at Kevin harshly, "I didn't pay for you to go to college to talk like that."

I instantly regretted it. Whatever I was seeing in Kevin, I wanted to control. I wanted Kevin to get back to normal, even though I knew "normal," from before the accident, would never happen. But still, the roller coaster was hard. There were days when Kevin seemed back to his normal, before-the-accident self; then others, like sitting at the restaurant, where he was someone entirely different. Every time I thought I had a handle on Kevin's new realities, I would be challenged with something else.

Later, Kevin told his rehab counselor about the incident, who then called Danny and I into her office. She confronted me.

"He can't help talking with an accent, and he doesn't need you to point it out."

The scolding was too much. She was accusing his mother and an eleven-year-old of having no empathy for Kevin's suffering, yet it was she who had none for us. No matter how many patients she saw or case studies she read, she would never understand the hell we had all been enduring.

Still, shame over rode my rage, and both Danny and I burst into tears. We knew when his counselor told us he couldn't help talking with an accent that Kevin would never be back to himself. It was more than the embarrassment of being confronted, it was that one statement that confirmed our worst fear: Kevin was never going to be the same. My heart ached, and a nagging feeling that this was all my fault would not leave me. It had been my job to protect Kevin from being hurt, and I had failed. I was the only parent; it was up to me to keep Kevin safe.

I didn't know then that what I was experiencing had a name: ambiguous loss. It's a hard thing to describe. It's a loss, but one that is unclear, like with Alzheimer's. With Alzheimer's, the person can be physically in the room, but they might not remember your name. They may be physically present, but psychologically absent. There is both, paradoxically, an absence and a presence. For us, Kevin was Kevin one minute, and not Kevin the next. Part of him died the day of this injury, yet he was physically with us, too, enjoying the Mariner's game and bullshitting about all the player's stats.

I didn't know whether to mourn the Kevin I knew or not. Some days I would feel grief for the Kevin I had known all his life—I tried to accept the new normal, the new Kevin. Then other days, he would come downstairs and offer up deep, intelligent insights about dynamics he noticed with friends or family. His insightfulness would lure me into telling myself he was fine.

Life was so unpredictable. My feelings were bouncing all over the place. I was still so afraid of Kevin dying that I was killing myself in an effort to keep him alive. Somehow, I believed that if I tried to control everything, including his accent, I could fix him. And I wanted him fixed so I didn't have to feel this pain. So I didn't have to sit with the powerlessness of this senseless tragedy. And so that I didn't have to feel the unbearable loss of Kevin as he was. I wanted to fight the accent because the accent was evidence of the loss of Kevin and life as we knew it.

It had never been about the accent. But how do you explain that to a therapist who has just shamed you in their office?

So, I doubled up my efforts to search for answers, support, and the right doctors. I soldiered on, keeping my eyes focused on the next right thing to do for Kevin. It was better than feeling all of the pain. There was no time for me in any of this. My feelings were an unnecessary indulgence in all of this. I collapsed in bed at night from exhaustion, and when I couldn't hold back the pain anymore, I would cry silently into my pillow before falling asleep.

Fortunately, I met a woman at a wedding who worked with people with brain injuries. She had heard about Kevin's accident from my sister-in-law, so she approached me. I talked in general about how Kevin was doing, and I mentioned the accent, how it troubled me, and embarrassed me.

"Kevin needs the accent to organize his brain," she explained to me. "It most likely helps him structure his thoughts and form them into some order so he can communicate." She explained how normal this behavior was for brain injury survivors.

Right there in the middle of all the celebration, I almost wept at her empathy. She explained with compassion; there was not a shred of judgment in what she was saying. Finally, it felt like I could make sense of it. I had a reason. If only I had been given this explanation earlier, if someone could have told me this sooner, we could have reduced so much stress, anxiety, and pain.

Interaction after interaction with the healthcare providers servicing Kevin got me thinking about the narrow focus of our healthcare system. I knew Kevin's rehab team was focusing on Kevin, and I was grateful for their care, but we, Kevin's family, were in distress too. We needed help, support, explanations, and comfort. But we weren't considered the patient, and therefore no services were provided. Wouldn't it improve the lives of TBI patients and their families if they were included in the recovery? I fought hard for his doctors to listen and work together, but it was to no avail. They were listening only to the perspective of someone with a brain injury who did not have full command of their mental abilities. My input would have clarified many things for them, making their jobs easier. Later in this recovery journey, Kevin and I were invited to be guests on a panel that included TBI patients and their parents to speak before a group of residents at the UC Davis Medical Center. Kevin talked about his recovery openly. I implored the doctors at the gathering to listen to the family, get signed releases, include them in the patient's care, and work together as a team, for the patient's overall success.

The hardest thing to realize—and it wasn't until after Kevin died that I came across this information—is what happens to a person's sense of self when they have a traumatic brain injury. To paraphrase Phyllis S. Kosminsky in "Loss of Functionality: Traumatic Brain Injury" from *Counting Our Losses: Reflecting on Change, Loss, and Transition in Everyday Life*, a person with a traumatic brain injury loses a sense of who they are, their identity, and their place in the world. Kosminsky calls it "the deepest insult to a person's sense of self." She states the injury is all encompassing, impacting every area of functioning, including loss of memory, changes in personality they cannot control, difficulties in processing information, and in communication. The loss of short-term memory is usually the most impactful because they often can't recall what they did the day before or even the morning before. Then, like a cascading wave, these changes impact every relationship they have.

Connection to others is so vital for self-esteem. People with TBI often experience a deep sense of loneliness because they cannot connect fully with others. It's not just the loss of function. They live with an injury that no one can see therefore no one gets what they are going through, and as a result, they feel misunderstood and misperceived. To top it off they face an uncertain future with employment, disability, and their relationships. This causes an incredible amount of stress and anxiety for the suffering patient which does not help create the best healing environment for the brain. There is so much loss for the patient and the family. So much unprocessed grief.

Much like learning the reasons behind Kevin's adaptation with the accent, this new information about people with TBI losing their sense of self made so much sense to me, and I desperately wished I had known about it earlier in Kevin's recovery. I wasn't blind to his emotional struggles; I just didn't know how to grasp the full picture of how the brain injury could so fundamentally relate to his self-esteem, especially since Kevin would shift between his old self and his new one.

If I had known . . . it's a dark phrase, but true, nonetheless. If I could go back in time, and if I couldn't erase the accident itself, then I would have focused so much more on trying to help him build up his self-esteem.

I remember when he first got home from the hospital, the year of rehabilitation still ahead of him, tears poured down his cheek as he discussed the accident. "This seems like such an unfair consequence for one night of drinking."

Drinking with the guys. Falling accidentally. Becoming permanently disabled. He was right. It was unfair. He didn't deserve it. Nobody did.

"It is," I replied. Grief seeped through the cracks. I wanted to cry with him, though I didn't. Inside, my heart was breaking into a million pieces, but I just let him cry.

Life can be cruel, as the saying goes, but never had I lived that reality so intimately. I had seen others suffer terrible things, but I had never experienced a tragedy of this magnitude on a personal level.

Little did I know how, just over a decade later, the tragedy would be compounded.

Kevin tried, though. As hard as life was for him, as much as he struggled to come to terms with his deficits and learn how to cope, he kept persevering.

One morning, Kevin decided to take the light rail into Sacramento just to hang out and be on his own. He was craving his favorite pizza from his favorite pizza joint, Giovanni's, and he had a craving to do it on his own. He made it as far as downtown, but misplaced his ticket, so they kicked him off the light rail. He had to call me to pick him up. It was just so heart crushing to hear his frustration and disappointment over the phone. Despite his best efforts to communicate with the ticket collector, he had failed. Despite the effort it took for this one little thing he tried to get back to himself, he had failed. Kevin wanted so badly to get a foothold in the normal world again, and this was yet another hurtful setback. Yet, to his credit, he tried again.

This time, he was able to make the trip to Sacramento to see a friend. His friend told me later it was one of hardest things he'd ever done, to put Kevin back on the light rail by himself. As he watched his face disappear down the tracks, he was overwhelmed by Kevin's current state of vulnerability that was caused by the loss of function and independence. But, much to everyone's relief, Kevin made it home.

It was a huge success.

As Kevin worked on his cognitive skills in outpatient rehab, I began to see him progressing in other ways, and it was my lifeline. Kevin quickly grabbed on to the words and skills they were teaching him after the initial frustration, but his brain was still not fully integrated. It was patchy, to say the least. Some parts worked fine; other parts were damaged. I knew that cognitively, yet on the outside, Kevin was looking better and better.

One evening, John, Kevin, Danny, and I were driving home after grabbing something to eat. I don't remember what I said or even how I said it, perhaps I was snapping but I don't recall anything out of the ordinary. We didn't exchange a lot of words. What I do remember is that when John pulled the car to a stop in the driveway, Kevin jumped out of the car before it stopped rolling and stormed off into the darkness of the night.

"Kevin!" I yelled from the front seat of the car, stunned. *What had I said that would elicit a reaction such as this?* He kept walking until I lost sight of him.

My heart began to race and I felt sick to my stomach, nothing I had said would have warranted this strong of a reaction from him. Kevin had such an easy-going personality before his accident, and up to this point, we had been focused on recovery. It was mostly positive, though those moments of frustration when he couldn't make his brain work could be brutal. But no matter how difficult, that frustration had always been directed at his broken brain; he had never directed his anger toward me. Now, it seemed, he was having angry outbursts that sprung up from misunderstandings caused by misinterpreting what had been said. And no matter the logic, Kevin could not be convinced otherwise, because he just couldn't process it. These interactions never ceased to shock me. As we began combing through the neighborhood, once again, in the total darkness, I was beginning to understand the changes in mood and outbursts of anger were all a result of having difficulty in processing information. Irritability was a regular visitor in our conversations as a different personality began to emerge. I never knew what to expect and neither did Kevin. Reflecting over it now as I write, I can only imagine his fear.

But we didn't know. We simply didn't know.

John took the car and drove around the nearby neighborhoods searching for him, leaving me anxiously waiting by the door. It had only been a few minutes, so he couldn't have gone far. As my eyes strained to make out Kevin's shadow, I kept thinking about his escape from the hospital and our needle-in-the-haystack search party. Panic began growing in my stomach as I realized how cold it was getting.

John found him about forty-five minutes later and brought him home. I tried to apologize to him, to smooth things over, to make it all okay. I didn't even know what I was apologizing for. Kevin didn't respond. He went to bed. Still angry.

Personality changes. A new issue. A new grief. Another loss. How much more could I take? I was grieving the loss of my son. Kevin, the version of the man that I had given birth to thirty years ago, died that day when he fell out of the truck. He was not the same. And no matter how many doctors' appointments or rehab sessions he went to, he would never be who and what he was before. I wanted to scream in a primal burst from the rooftop. I wanted everybody near and far to hear my anguish. *Kevin's not the same! Kevin is dead! How am I going to survive without him? Who was this version of my son? How was I going to relate to him?*

Kevin was so unpredictable it was like walking on eggshells trying not to upset him. And I was only human too. I wasn't perfect. It was impossible never to make a mistake or say the wrong thing, especially since no one knew what the right or wrong things were. I didn't know what I was up against. I had no road map. There were no steps I could look at or stages to identify. This was simply, sadly, irreversibly, because his brain was not working the same way.

The next morning, Kevin got up and came downstairs. I tensed up as I poured myself a cup of coffee, not sure which version of Kevin I was going to get. He smiled at me as he said good morning and headed to the refrigerator to get the cream for his coffee. I breathed out a sigh of relief as I took another sip of coffee. All was well. He wasn't mad at me. Strangely, everything seemed fine. Maybe with his short-term memory loss he had forgotten. Yet for me, I was still reeling with emotion because I hadn't forgotten. But I'd take this Kevin today. It was the Kevin I knew.

CHAPTER 15
Deficits

"You know, twenty years ago, you would have died."

Dr. Portwood was conducting a post rehab follow up exam testing Kevin's brain function. She leaned back in her chair, amazed, reflecting on the years she had worked with TBI patients. Kevin had just completed a series of complex math problems without hesitation, answering immediately AND correctly. Kevin was always brilliant at math, so I wasn't surprised. He could have solved those problems before the brain injury, but given how unpredictable his recovery had been, I was definitely impressed too. As I watched him work through the problems, I couldn't help but remember him as a fourth grader, and how excited we had both been when he was placed in the Johns Hopkins Math Program for gifted children at Arizona State University at the time. Often, his teachers would think he cheated on tests because he did his math in his head without showing his work. His mind was like a calculator. Dr. Portwood herself was stunned by Kevin's capability to do these complex math problems after such a significant brain injury.

Dr. Portland had seen Kevin in the early stages of his brain injury in the acute rehab. She had been with us through the escape from the hospital and was the doctor who discharged him to return home. Kevin had made a remarkable recovery in her opinion. It was during these appointments that I experienced the back-and-forth whiplash of hope. Here, I was encouraged; my grief was quieted. I'd go home believing maybe Kevin could fully recover. I'd fall asleep that night, reminded that maybe there was a light at the end of this dark tunnel after all.

As days turned into months, I immersed myself into not only how the human brain worked, but how Kevin's brain worked. I was still learning so much. Neuroplasticity gave his brain the capacity to rewire itself and create new pathways, thereby making new connections, resulting in learning new abilities. Other parts of Kevin's brain were not damaged at all, specifically the back of Kevin's brain. According to his doctor, this part of the brain was where complex math problems could be figured out, which is why Kevin never lost the ability to know basketball facts or baseball player's statistics. He could quote the stats on any player. It was incredible, and I was so grateful for that, given his love of sports.

All the math comprehension and basketball stats were great, but not really affecting Kevin's day-to-day overall success. What was so devastating was the loss of social cues, his struggle with controlling his emotions, and the suffering that came with sleep deprivation, since a head injury often results in disruptions to your sleep pattern. He suffered from ongoing chronic pain in his head and back. He lost short-term memory. He had difficulty processing paperwork or sometimes would trail off mid-conversation. But he kept trying. Always, he kept trying. Despite his neurological challenges, Kevin remained a deep thinker with incredible insight, and was also very loving. He would often send messages to us out of the blue: *Love you buddy*. I could cry right now, just thinking about that.

His friends would often rely on Kevin's perspective for many of their issues in life, even after his accident. So did some of my family members, including me. Kevin had a rare capacity to have presence, compassion, and insight. When you talked to Kevin, you felt he met you, that he was right there. His insight was evidence that he heard you and understood you. He was present. In today's world, this is a rare and uniquely beautiful thing.

Kevin had never been an aggressive person. He was easy going, a go-with-the-flow kind of guy. Even when his favorite team lost a championship, he would remain emotionally steady, while tensions went high. So, it was all the more startling to see the changes in his behavior as he became angrier and more aggressive.

"I feel like a cornered animal," Kevin once told me about how he experienced his anger.

It was the fight-or-flight response, clearly. A cornered animal wants to lash out to protect themselves, they want to defend against the attacker. Kevin sensed danger everywhere. *Attack, fight back*, his brain would tell him. In the immediate moment of a real or imagined threat, Kevin became angry because he'd lost his ability to use his higher-level brain. He never threw things, nor did he ever hit anyone, but nonetheless, his aggression could be intimidating.

One night, when Kevin still lived with us, he got angry that he was in the kitchen doing the dishes after dinner.

"No one told you to do them," I replied as he scrubbed a dinner plate in a huff.

"You're living with us for free," John snapped at him watching as the entire argument began to unfold. I made eye contact with John and tried to communicate that he needed to be quiet. John was still expecting Kevin to respond to life as a person who had a fully functioning brain would. Many people did. It was extraordinarily confusing to see Kevin looking normal and even acting normal sometimes, and then be confronted with uncharacteristic anger. John, of course, was looking at the situation from the perspective of someone who was helping

Kevin in every way he could, yet still, it seemed like for Kevin, it wasn't enough. Without understanding Kevin's deficits, John felt purposely unappreciated.

Kevin snapped back at John, angry, hostile words spewing from his mouth. John, still angry himself, spun around and stormed out into the backyard, even as Kevin continued to do the dishes. But Kevin couldn't let it go and so he rushed outside to continue the confrontation. Kevin ran up to him, thrust his chest toward John, indicating he was going to chest bump him. I gasped, shocked at Kevin's threatening actions.

As if realizing this was not a fair fight John backed off. "It gets bloody when grown men fight," he seethed in Kevin's direction.

That was enough to get Kevin to disengage, but still the incident frightened me. Not so much that it would resort to violence, but how different Kevin had become. I felt helpless.

Kevin started blowing up at all of us as he walked back into the house. Kara, who was visiting with us at the time, managed to get him out of the house and into her car. Terrified, I followed them to the driveway and tried to talk to him, desperately hoping I could calm him down, but he was seething with anger.

Danny had run out of the house with me, scared too. He couldn't understand what was happening with his brother, why he was suddenly threatening violence. Danny searched Kevin's face looking for clues that this was really his brother.

Kevin's hostile behavior toward John, Danny's father, destroyed their relationship for a long time. Despite the large age gap, they had always been brothers, not strangers, not acquaintances, but family. With Kevin's newly surfaced aggression—that none of us could properly understand—Danny was angry with Kevin and had a lot of trouble forgiving him.

Eventually, Kevin calmed down. He came back inside, but John and Kevin would continue to keep their distance from each other. For years, I would try, unsuccessfully, to explain to John what I understood about Kevin's head injury. But he didn't believe it; he didn't want to. It would have meant feeling all the loss and sorrow, and he just couldn't go there. It was safer to believe Kevin had control of his actions and was choosing these behaviors than it was to reconcile that part of his brain was so damaged he would regularly be reduced to functioning like an angry toddler. I knew where he was coming from—the last thing I wanted to feel was that very loss and sorrow, the grief, the ambiguous loss, but I didn't have a choice. Kevin needed me to accept it so he could move on.

So, when Kevin's neurologist asked me to come into an appointment, I agreed. I was blindsided when the doctor confronted me for the way John had treated Kevin during the conflict. "It's not a fair fight with a brain-injured person who doesn't have the full capacity of his brain."

"I agree," I tried to explain. "I didn't like John's response either, but I understood it. We're all doing our best here. In fairness to John, he does support Kevin financially and lets him live with us for free. He tries to help Kevin as best as he knows how. He's not a bad person."

"Oh," the doctor answered, relenting.

I sighed. It was always like this. Kevin could only tell part of the story; the doctor seemed to have missed the rest. It reminded me how we needed the medical system to adapt better for TBI patients. By definition, they were incapacitated in some way, so why not make it easier for family members to be involved in their care? If I had been able to explain the whole conflict to the doctor, we would have had clearer communication right from the start.

As it was, the incident led the neurologist to recognize that Kevin was having mini seizures (abnormal electrical activity in the brain), which is typical following an injury like his. Since they did not appear as grand mal seizures with violent muscle contractions or loss of consciousness, these mini seizures went unnoticed. No one could witness the seizures to identify something was wrong, yet it was the seizures that were impacting his brain and causing Kevin to feel irritable and aggressive. The neurologist started him on seizure medication and an antidepressant, Lexapro, and together, these medications calmed his brain which led to significant improvement in his anger and less outbursts.

I was both frustrated and relieved. It was yet another sign that Kevin would never be "back to normal," but at least he and John weren't duking it out in the backyard anymore. I'd have to take the wins where I could get them.

But that win was short lived after another incident at his doctor's office where he'd become frustrated at not being able to communicate with the staff. Kevin had gotten angry, and the doctor had refused to treat him. Kevin was crushed, because he'd really liked that doctor, but it also helped Kevin realize he needed more help. He found a neuropsychologist who specialized in traumatic brain injuries and anger management.

"Assume you'll always be angry with your TBI," he said. "Live with the expectation that this will be a daily issue."

Always be angry? Another loss. If this were a sports game and Kevin were keeping score, it didn't look like he was ever going to catch up. We had to face the fact that Kevin would never again regain his easy-going personality.

Regardless of the realities, Kevin did learn tools for managing his anger, and he improved significantly. In fact, Kevin improved so much, there were whole entire days where he was just himself, easy-going, good-natured, the one who didn't get flustered. Given how people with fully functioning brains can't often control their anger, what Kevin was doing was heroic.

But it was also just another loop on the roller coaster. Up one day, down the next.

I didn't know how bad it was. John would say years later.

Our sense of ourselves originates from interactions we have with others in our environment, yet a person surviving TBI experiences these interactions in an acutely different way, and their sense of self is shattered when people just don't understand. What if we had known?

What if all of us had known?

We are hardwired for connection, yet Kevin's connections had been broken the moment he landed on his head.

I often felt alone in dealing with Kevin because no one else close to him wanted to acknowledge the realities. It would have been more fixable if he was struggling with drug addiction because that was mainstream. I know it's a form of self-preservation, but the emotional distancing that inevitably happened with our family felt like a great abandonment of me too. Being willing to see the truth is a lonely experience.

For a time, things settled down. Kevin was taking the proper medication and still doing therapy, and I think he really felt back to himself. It was just over a year since the accident, and Kara and Matt were long-term house-sitting for our next door neighbors while they were in England. I loved having them next door. All my kids were within my reach, and my sweet grandson Jack was right next door too.

Kara and Kevin had always been close growing up, though of course, Kevin hadn't been exactly thrilled to have a new baby sister— like most kids he had loved having me all to himself for the first seven years of his life. But over time, the two became buddies, bonding over our Friday night dinners at Someburros Mexican restaurant before walking around the mall to windowshop. Kevin taught Kara how to throw and catch a football; he would spend hours with her, forcing her to catch the football one hundred times in a row, without dropping it. If she dropped it, the count started all over again from one, and she loved every minute of it. Kara would go on to impress the boys in high school with her football skills. They always expected this cute, little cheerleader to be clueless about the sport, but when she played powder-puff football, she mowed them over with her amazing skills. Kevin and Kara also bonded deeply over the absence of their fathers; it seems I had chosen men who chose not to be involved in their kids' lives. They didn't have their dads, but they had each other, and that was worth a lot. Kevin was not only a big brother to Kara, but at times, he was a father figure to her as well. He was the only dependable male figure in her life until I married John when Kevin was sixteen and Kara was nine.

When Kara married Matt, we all noticed how similar Matt and Kevin were in their looks and their love of sports. Matt and Kevin were close to the same age, so they, too, became friends. They had an ease to their relationship, and they had a big thing in common: they both loved Kara. On this particular beautiful, sunny California day, Kevin, Kara, and Matt were sitting outside preparing for the BBQ they had invited us to. The sun was warm, but not unbearable, and it felt perfect on my skin. Perfect weather. Perfect family. I sighed in contentment as I looked at all three of my children and my grandson around the patio table. We had survived this awful year. Kevin was his normal happy self: relaxed, talkative, and telling jokes. *How lucky are we?* I kept thinking as I helped Kara bring the side dishes from the kitchen to the outside.

Kara noticed too; she was so full of joy, the contentment lit up her face. Her smile was peaceful and seemed to suggest that all was right with the world. Kevin and Matt were connecting like the good ole days, and John and I were relaxed enough to focus on chatting while Danny played close by. Jack was just a toddler sitting on the ground playing with his toys. It was so normal. It had been such a long time. It was moments like this that we had longed for in the nightmare days of the ICU and acute rehab. In that moment, with Kevin present and himself, it seemed like he had beaten TBI. We all wanted to believe we had our happily-ever-after story.

And for that day, we did.

CHAPTER 16
A Crushing Realization

Kevin made incredible progress in a year of post outpatient rehabilitation, so his rehab team recommended he return to work. Before the accident, Kevin had worked as an estimator for John's roofing company, and had done so since he graduated from college. His job was to deal with construction plans and bid work based on the calculations he estimated for the roof. Kevin did his job with ease when he started at the company; he liked numbers and winning contracts. In fact, Kevin proved quite successful when he showed an aptitude for connecting to other contractors—the builders loved him and so did his colleagues. Kevin especially loved the male camaraderie at work. He was always up for lunch with different suppliers or just the guys from the office. Kevin had been the main estimator at the time of his accident and loved feeling like the expert. A younger estimator, Roy, had been added to the team and part of his responsibility was to train Roy. Ironically, Roy had been one of the men with Kevin the night of his accident. While Kevin was out of work, learning how to soap himself in the shower and read on a kindergarten level, Roy continued to gain estimating skills and superseded what Kevin would be able to do when he went back. It was a blow to Kevin's self-esteem.

Before Kevin returned to work, the rehab team met with John to discuss accommodations. They even visited John at work to get a clearer picture of what Kevin might need to be gainfully employed. As his stepfather, John was willing to bring him back to the company, but no one could foresee the problems that would develop. John never seemed to fully understand Kevin's limitations, or maybe he didn't want to accept them because it would mean facing Kevin was permanently disabled. He would tell me years later, that he had never truly appreciated just how disabled Kevin had been. It was heart-wrenching and validating to hear all at the same time.

Though he was back to living independently in his own apartment, and he was still capable of doing a bid and securing certain jobs for the company, the work would exhaust Kevin's brain, requiring him to sleep for days to recover. And it didn't help matters that he also had a sleep disorder.

Sleep disturbance is an incapacitating problem for brain injured people. Lack of sleep meant Kevin could not show up for work the next day. We tried to set up a system for Kevin to call, even in the middle of the night, if he realized his sleep would be disrupted. It helped John to know if Kevin was going to be at work or not. Eventually Kevin's doctor put him on sleep medication, which only helped half the time. When they did take effect, Kevin would be drugged so deeply by these powerful sleeping pills that he wouldn't be able to call in as a result.

Kevin's frustration at his inability to perform at the level he had worked at before the injury, coupled with the fact that his trainee and friend, Roy, had surpassed him in ability, led Kevin to act out and become very angry and hostile. Some days he sent John angry emails laced with curse words. When John instituted a program where an estimator could get a bonus for securing other jobs, Kevin became even more disgruntled. He was unable to manage it all. Estimating requires several little tasks that involve executive functioning skills like interpreting the plans, and then calculating the numbers for the bid. It overwhelmed him.

I felt torn. I hated that Kevin became so hostile toward John— he was just trying to run his business that supported his family, and obviously he needed his employees at full strength, but on the other hand, it was obvious Kevin wasn't well. Though he might have appeared recovered, I knew he wasn't, and it frustrated me that John couldn't see it the same way. In reality, it was hard to see because Kevin looked normal and was acting normal most of the time. Still, it was business, and the two of them would have to work something out.

It was a long, difficult process. John wanted to help Kevin but also needed a reliable worker. Kevin's energy level and ability to complete tasks were unpredictable. John saw how much Kevin was struggling to keep up with the workload and acknowledged that. While Kevin was off work, the company had expanded and completely changed. Jim was gone and a new boss was in his place—Kevin was never returning to the job or the company he knew—it was a whole different playing field, and his new boss wasn't very kind or compassionate. Kevin felt he was constantly putting him down and criticizing him. Eventually, the job became the main thing that was damaging Kevin's already fragile self-esteem. Kevin felt betrayed by John who he did not believe was standing up for him to his new partner. John was just trying to run the business. It was a mess.

One day, after Kevin didn't show up to work, I went to his apartment to check on him. I knew Kevin was still hurt and angry, believing John chose his new partner over him. He felt as his stepson he should have been a priority. He was family, and John should have been on his side.

I had to say I agreed with Kevin.

"What about stepping away? Go to vocational rehabilitation and find a new career?" I suggested. We sat silently for a minute. I could see the toll all of this was taking on both of them. "Let John figure out this guy is an asshole. Remove yourself. It's not your responsibility. "

I still hoped John could work out a place for Kevin at the company, but I could see it was hard for both of them. John had to grow his company to keep going; the work environment was too fast paced and demanding for Kevin's brain—he needed something calmer where he could have fewer tasks and more independence. He was still very bright even with the head injury. Kevin considered my suggestion, but he was in a new relationship and didn't want to believe he couldn't be a productive employee.

It was a tumultuous time, yet we kept striving. John, Kevin, and I even went to discuss the work challenges with Kevin's neuropsychologist who tried to tell us Kevin wasn't being heard. Now, looking back, it hurts my heart to realize the psychologist was right, that I too, had not really listened to Kevin. As much as I tried to see Kevin's perspective, I did think his brain injury was playing a part in Kevin's view of this new boss. Sadly, John, too, ignored Kevin's perspective, invalidating it because of his brain injury, thinking Kevin was just angry that he couldn't perform as he had in the past.

Ultimately, John did learn Kevin was right about his partner, but it was a long time in coming. His business partner went on to struggle with several other employees. Finally, John was on the receiving end of this person's behavior and realizing how right Kevin had been, he regretted dismissing Kevin at that time.

As fate would have it, John's company was going through some financial struggles during the recession of 2008 so he needed to lay off some of his employees. Kevin was one of the workers who was laid off, which gave him time to look for other employment options.

I had always been Kevin's support person, and I'd always been someone who focused on the next step; despite the stormy waters we had to navigate, I was going to keep doing both. I found out how to get Kevin evaluated for vocational rehabilitation, a program that attempts to help disabled people find employment. They might train a client in a new occupation or assist them in finding work that matched their abilities. Kevin applied for the program and was accepted. He was put through a battery of psychological and occupational tests over several days. In the meantime, I began helping Kevin fill out paperwork for permanent disability just in case. The conclusion of the testing was that Kevin had difficulty multitasking, difficulty with memory, and difficulty processing directions. The team realized holding a job down would be extremely difficult for Kevin and so they supported my decision to move forward with the permanent disability claim. It wasn't the perfect solution, but it was going to be the best one for Kevin. In addition to getting on disability, Kevin would receive healthcare which he desperately needed since he had so many health problems related to TBI, including a back injury he sustained in the fall.

It was a crushing realization that Kevin would never again be the Kevin, not just in mind but body too, from before the accident. In the hospital, the doctor had told us to expect deficits; at the time we had no idea what that meant. Now, we were becoming aware of just how fundamentally Kevin's life had changed.

John wrote a letter on Kevin's behalf for the disability claim documenting what they call a failed work experience. He had tried to return to work, and it failed. The testing and the letter helped Kevin secure permanent disability after an eighteen-month application process. If it was hard for me to see Kevin's life altered so drastically, it was an even more bitter pill for Kevin to swallow. On the one hand, Kevin knew work was difficult for him; he recognized his limitations even if it was hard for him to admit them. He especially recognized the difficulty with sleep, how it would interfere in his ability to show up to a job on time, and work a regular shift. Kevin wanted to work, make money, and be successful. He wanted to get back on the track he was humming along on before the accident. In the moments of deepest struggle, Kevin would share with me that the brain injury had made him humble because he had to rely on God for everything, every day. Whether it was a simple task or dealing with the debilitating chronic pain, he could no longer move through any of it without the miracle of help from a power greater than himself. The brain injury had completely changed his world view. He wasn't in charge, and the need to accept that in order to move on was as jarring emotionally as the chronic pain was physically. In one moment of lost balance, his dreams collapsed in front of him.

But, Kevin wasn't just a person with a head injury who couldn't work and had nothing to offer. He was loving and kind and intelligent even with the TBI. Kevin could not be defined just by his value to perform at work. He had much more to offer especially in loving relationships. Before he was laid off, Kevin had started dating and planned to get married. As much as the decision to go on disability was a blow to him, we believed there was still room for hope that Kevin would recover more fully. It seemed Kevin's life was improving in some areas even as he faced this crushing blow.

CHAPTER 17

Happily Ever After

The farmer's market in El Dorado Hills was one of our favorite summertime activities. The strawberries were always ruby-red delicious, and every time I sank my teeth into one, I couldn't help but think that eating their strawberries was better than any candy. The tomatoes sold at the grocery store could never compare to the organic tomatoes sold at the market, and the peaches, oh my, the peaches. I can almost taste them now, even as I write. Kevin loved the mouth-watering strawberries, and while I was a frequent shopper at the market, Kara and Matt went weekly without fail. Kara would often invite Kevin along for something to do. About a year and a half after the accident, they were at the market, and Kevin noticed a very attractive Mexican woman working in one of the berry stands.

"She's really pretty," Kevin commented to Kara. As he picked through the containers of fruit.

His sister jumped on it. "Go over and talk to her!" she encouraged.

"About what?"

Kara huffed good-naturedly. "Just ask about the fruits and vegetables."

Kevin took a deep breath, walked over, and pretended to check out the tomatoes before switching to the berries.

"How much do the blackberries cost? Three dollars?" he inquired.

He was surprised at the price so Lorena made him an offer.

"You can have two for five dollars."

Long after Lorena and Kevin were married, the moment would become a popular, heartwarming family story. Kevin hated tomatoes. And they both liked a bargain.

It was September 19, 2009.

Kevin returned the next week, same time, same stand, and gathered all his courage and asked Lorena for her phone number.

"I have two children," she replied cautiously.

"I like kids," Kevin replied, hopefully.

Kevin was a natural with children, given the big family I come from, plus all the grandkids—we were a very kid-oriented family. It was what Kevin knew, what he'd grown up with, and he loved it.

"Okay," Lorena answered hesitantly, "But I don't want a boyfriend."

They went on their first date shortly after.

In spite of her protests that she didn't want a serious boyfriend, Kevin hit it off with Lorena, and her two kids. Ozzie was two years old; Carmen was five. Kevin adored them immediately, always getting down on the floor to play with them, and they, too, fell in love with Kevin. Kevin always treated Ozzie like his own son. He paraded him around everywhere they went. The first time I met Lorena and her children was at mass on a Sunday at the Cathedral of the Blessed Sacrament in Sacramento. Kevin had been holding Ozzie up proudly showing him off, and he was very sweetly protective of Carmen too.

Connecting to Lorena's family was so good for Kevin. It gave him some normality and joy, and he loved it. Though Kevin tried to explain his brain injury to Lorena, she didn't really see it. Since his disability was invisible, she only saw that Kevin was very smart and capable. In one way, we could see this was a good thing. Since Lorena hadn't known Kevin before the accident, she would often expect more of him, which pushed him to do more too. But it was also a detriment because she didn't understand how all his deficits impacted his life and would eventually impact hers. A lot of heartache would come from her misunderstandings; she would later come to blame Kevin for things over which he had no control, but even in retrospect, I can't fully blame her. If Kevin's own doctors, family, including me, at times, couldn't quite wrap our heads around just what deficits Kevin was constrained by and when, I could appreciate how hard it was for Lorena. She could see only an able-bodied individual capable of so, so much. She wasn't wrong—Kevin had come a long way since the day of the accident—but sadly, there was so much she missed too.

Lorena wanted to get married, and she put a deadline on their relationship. Kevin had very little money but managed to scrape together enough to buy her a real diamond ring. He had wanted so badly to get her a larger ring, but I reassured him she would be happy to get engaged. Maybe a bigger ring could be purchased in the future.

Kevin had plans to take Lorena to the farmer's market in El Dorado Hills where they had first met to propose. Anxiety and excitement got the better of him, so he asked her one night when she was cooking in the kitchen. They danced in each other's arms the rest of the night. They were both so happy.

This was about the time that working for John was becoming increasingly difficult for Kevin; the strain was building, and the writing was on the wall. It wouldn't be long before he was on disability, but for that moment, his engagement to Lorena was full of joy. When she and Kevin stopped by the next day, and Lorena flashed her ring, I jumped out of my chair. I was so excited for them! I had known Kevin had the ring; I just hadn't expected he would give it to her the night he did, but I was so happy for them. After so much heartache, pain, and unending obstacles, Kevin deserved this happiness. It made our celebrations all that much more poignant.

Lorena set up a wedding date for August so her children could enroll in the local schools in Folsom where they planned to live. Since her own mother wasn't in the country, Lorena asked me to go shopping with her for her wedding dress. I was more than happy to oblige.

Lorena had a rough upbringing. After discovering she was pregnant at age fifteen, her boyfriend pressured her to cross the border from Mexico into the United States so their baby could be a US citizen. And then, her boyfriend dumped her. Here she was, a new mother by the age of sixteen without adequate English language skills and she had to survive. Trust was hard-won with her, and despite how her own childhood issues affected her relationship with Kevin, I still have a lot of respect for her.

Lorena found the perfect dress and veil, they got the church, and everything was moving forward.

About a month before the wedding, Kevin's work crisis peaked. He knew he couldn't keep working for John, and, because of the economy, John had to lay some people off, so he let Kevin go. Though Kevin had unemployment insurance, Lorena was concerned. She later told me that her mother, who lived in Mexico, encouraged her to marry Kevin so she wouldn't have to work, but now that Kevin had left his job, it scared her. She and Kevin loved each other, but given her own upbringing, financial security was important to her. She finally reasoned that because Kevin was a hard worker and he had a college degree, he'd find another job. Of course, what she hadn't expected—what none of us had expected—was Kevin's permanent inability to keep a job. While Kevin was laid off, he was tested for vocational rehabilitation. The test results concluded Kevin would have extreme difficulty holding a job, so the determination was made to move forward with permanent disability. It was devastating for Kevin, but crushing for Lorena, too, especially when she didn't really understand the invisible constraints of Kevin's brain injury. Still, holding onto her fragile hopes of what she wanted their lives to look like, she moved forward with the wedding. They rented a house in a quiet neighborhood of Folsom and settled down. It was going to be a sweet start to their new life together.

The wedding was beautiful, though the priest at the church was a little rigid, and he had trouble with some of the Mexican traditions. In the end, Lorena got to fulfill the customs important to her, such as draping the rosary around them both during the mass, and leaving flowers for the statue of Our Lady. My heart, broken so many times over the months since Kevin's accident, was put back together in some places. Kevin deserved this moment. We all did.

The reception, complete with Mexican food and margaritas, was full of life—such a juxtaposition of the last couple of years. The venue, an indoor/outdoor reception area, had lights twinkling dimly on one side, and a gorgeous sunset on the other. There was a DJ, music, dancing, and so much joy.

We did a lot of it ourselves, which made the wedding that much more intimate. We'd ordered Lorena's favorite wedding cake from a Mexican bakery, and Kevin's Aunt Mimi and Uncle Jim helped cut it. Uncle John helped with the drinks; we all pitched in for the clean-up, but none of it felt like work—it was a family affair we were proud to be a part of. Sadly, most of Lorena's family could not attend since they lived in Mexico, but her cousins and her friends showed up to bring the party.

For Kevin, for Lorena, it was a fairy tale.

And as Kevin's mom, who had started to believe that he was going to live out a very lonely existence in the aftermath of his accident, it was a fairy tale for me too.

But as with all fairy tales, the magic was short-lived.

CHAPTER 18

Pain

A few months into their wedded bliss, Kevin started experiencing paralyzing head pain. He would soon be prescribed Norco, a strong, opioid-based pain reliever. It would be the only way he could ever get out of bed; sadness and new challenges were beginning to emerge.

Kevin was struggling with chronic pain as a result of his head injury. He described it as a sharp pain that came on suddenly and so full of force that it made him weak in the knees. Lorena called me over one night because Kevin was suffering so badly, and she didn't know what to do. He dropped to his knees in front of me, grabbing his head between his two clenched hands, rocking back and forth, crying like a baby, whimpering that he couldn't take this pain. I had never witnessed anything like it. At the time, he had been prescribed, and was taking, Norco, but it didn't take long for us to realize it wasn't enough to interrupt the pain cycle.

"Get in the car. We are going to the ER," I told him sternly.

"They won't help me," he said, in between painful moans.

"Well, we have to at least try."

We went to the hospital, and Kevin explained to the ER nurse that he was in terrible pain and that he had run out of his pain medication. The nurse didn't believe him, which was made clear when he said, "I think you are just scamming for drugs."

I was shocked at his response. How could the nurse miss the obvious? Kevin wasn't putting on an act to get drugs. He needed prescription medication to control his very real pain.

I cut off the nurse in impatient anger, "I made him come; he didn't want to—he's not scamming for drugs." *What an insensitive, judgmental asshole*, I thought to myself.

Reluctantly, the nurse got him a bed in a room while we waited for care. Tears streamed down Kevin's cheeks, not just because of his physical suffering, but because he wasn't being believed. I was so angry at the injustice, and even more so when the next nurse came in to check Kevin's vitals. He, too, had the most judgmental attitude.

When a third nurse came in, I let her have it. I told her how furious I was at how Kevin was being treated. I explained the scene that had met me just hours before, him doubled over in pain, and how I had been the one to insist he come to the ER. I made it clear to them that he didn't want to come here for the very reasons that were happening: he knew he would be judged for needing pain medication. It galled me to think that the medical staff couldn't see that pain meds weren't all bad, that not everyone was a junkie, and that, yes, there were valid reasons someone would need pain medication. His only alternative was to curl up into a fetal position begging for relief. As I stared at him, wracked with pain, glued to the hospital bed, I couldn't help but feel overwhelmed by all the memories of the last couple of years. *What kind of life is this?* Kevin just wanted his life back.

The nurse I ranted to understood. She was sympathetic. "I have a friend with a traumatic brain injury who had terrible pain until it was managed by a doctor," she explained.

"Yes," I felt a surge of excitement well up inside me at the thought of being understood. "Kevin needs pain management." Not just pain medication.

But the system didn't work that way.

If only a team of doctors could have worked together to manage his pain . . .

But having at least one person, this one nurse in the ER, finally understand the real issue gave me so much relief that I almost cried. Someone got what he was going through. Someone understood he needed his pain managed, that his pain wasn't going to go away with a few pills on an as-needed basis.

Kevin was given pain medication that night in the ER and a few pills to get him through until he could see his doctor. When the pain medication kicked in, I could see the tension and pain slowly dissipate. I watched his head relax, then his shoulders, then the rest of his body seemed flooded with relief. He was able to walk out of the hospital, go home, and get some sleep.

I went home that night feeling that the whole situation felt hopeful, that he could have his pain managed. What a great concept, given that he would always have pain related to the injury. The next day, Kevin made an appointment to see Dr. Portwood, his doctor in the acute rehab, who specialized in pain management—something we didn't know when he saw her previously. She gave him another prescription for Norco. Eventually, Kevin was also prescribed oxycodone and OxyContin. Other doctors began prescribing pain medication too. Kevin had a primary care doctor who prescribed him pain medication at various times, as did other doctors on his team. Since none of the medical professionals were working together, no one really knew, holistically, how many drugs, including oxycodone, Kevin was being prescribed. I certainly didn't know they were handing them out like candy. And, shocking as it may seem now, the doctors at the time believed oxycodone wasn't addictive because it had a time release mechanism that titrated the amount of medication he was absorbing. On the outside, it looked like we were all witnessing pain relief. Kevin was able to get up out of bed and function in the world. Kevin was Kevin again, and since Kevin desperately wanted to gain a foothold in the non-brain-injured world, this seemed to be his ticket.

On the inside, Kevin's addiction was starting to take root.

At the same time, Kevin was receiving help from his neurologist for sleep. One of the most challenging problems following a head injury is difficulty sleeping. An injury to the brain disrupts the circadian sleep-wake rhythm resulting in chronic insomnia. Disturbed sleep further impacts a person's cognitive functioning and results in worsening short-term memory, depression, and irritability. Kevin was often getting very little sleep which would require him to stay in bed all day. The pain medicine helped him function, but the sleep deprivation was taking its toll. So, after failed attempts with other drugs like trazodone and Lunesta, the neurologist prescribed Ambien, a powerful sleep medication. Yet Ambien was another nightmare. Though it seemed to help a little, it still took hours for Kevin to fall asleep, leaving him feeling and appearing drugged. He would sit in a chair, eyes unable to focus, eating dry cereal or potato chips with his hands. He was so loopy he could barely get the food in his mouth, sometimes missing his mouth entirely. *Too much Ambien*, I thought, as I watched this scene unfold more than once. It was frightening. As a result of this nighttime overeating, Kevin began to gain weight.

In defense of the doctors who prescribed the medication, I could appreciate how hard it was to watch the level of suffering people have after an accident. The doctors wanted to do something. They wanted to help Kevin. They all genuinely wanted to give him relief so he could have a life. But no one understood that opioids that were not properly managed were not the solution.

Lorena called me one day to tell me she found Kevin passed out on a plate of food in the middle of the night. It's a miracle it didn't smother him to death. She cleaned him up and put him on the couch to sleep, but she was distressed. She didn't know what to do, and the only solution she could imagine was that Kevin stop all the medication. If the drugs were causing him such problems, then obviously getting rid of them was her solution.

"He doesn't need all these drugs," she cried on the other end of the phone.

I sat there silently. Half of me agreed, and yet none of us had to live with Kevin's pain. He did need the drugs—he just needed them managed appropriately. Yet when I wrote letters to all his doctors begging them to coordinate his care, only one doctor responded.

"This may be the best it gets for your son."

The best it gets?? Falling asleep in his food?

None of the other doctors responded, bound by confidentiality laws. I understood the concept, of course, and yes, Kevin was an adult, but he was brain-damaged; how could he adequately advocate for himself when parts of his brain weren't functioning properly?

Inevitably, Kevin became addicted to oxycodone. He crossed the line from use to abuse, we're just not sure when; there was no flashbulb, spotlight moment that let us all know he'd tipped over. It was a gradual decline, subtle. He simply began taking more of the medication than was prescribed. He was on Ambien, a seizure medication, Lexapro, and Norco or OxyContin and oxycodone. It was a pharmaceutical nightmare, and then he started drinking again. Kevin's behavior became even more unpredictable. The cycle of addiction coupled with the unpredictability of the brain injury created a roller coaster of emotions.

I tried. I tried so hard. I would cry, I would yell, I would beg, I would plead—with the doctors, with Kevin, with anybody, "Just listen!" Frantic, I felt powerless and alone. No one seemed to appreciate

Kevin's spiral in the same way I did. No one seemed to understand it wasn't simply about an addiction. Getting clean wouldn't serve Kevin, not the way we often think when it comes to addicts. I'd lived firsthand through Kevin's mounting pain; without some pain medication, he'd be as unable to function as too much pain medication was now making him. He needed a balance. He needed help figuring out what that balance was. But no one would listen.

I collapsed in tears one morning after checking my email and seeing I had zero responses from the doctors. How did this become my life? How had this devastation happened to that baby I loved so much? That adorable child so bright and full of promise—what had happened to him? And when, *when*, would I ever get him back?

In spite of all these issues with the pain medication and the TBI, Kevin enjoyed being a family man. In fact, the pain medication allowed him to have a life and be with his family. Family was the thing that kept him going. It gave him purpose. He loved picking the kids up from school, coaching their basketball and baseball teams, and cooking them dinner. His family was his world.

CHAPTER 19

Restraining Order

I'd heard chronic pain described as being not dead, but not alive either. And after seeing it firsthand—I can confidently say, it's a monster. It feeds on every waking moment and swallows up the sleeping moments too. As much as I wanted to, I couldn't absorb the pain of Kevin's problems. My own life was full of demands that had been piling up in the wake of Kevin's accident. But brain injuries don't care that you have other children to care for, or your own health and emotional wellness to consider. Brain injuries are no respecter of persons, and so they just keep hitting you with one crisis after another. I would always get nervous when a couple of days went by without any drama. I wasn't ever sure if it was because I had grown so accustomed to the tumult that had become my life, or if I was in tune enough to predict when another shoe was about to drop. It was on one such day when, out of the blue, I picked up my ringing phone and heard a panicked call from my youngest brother Paul. Paul was only three years older than Kevin and one of his best friends. "Kevin is so desperate that he wants to drive his car into a tree," he shouted into the phone before I finished saying hello. "He wants to die! He wants the pain to end!"

Blinking back tears, I didn't want to believe him. "Are you sure? I just spoke to him a few hours ago. He seemed . . . fine." My mind raced through our conversation. *Was he fine?*

"I'm scared, Brenda. I'm scared he's going to drive his car into a tree. He's not being rational. I can't talk to him."

I took a deep breath and decided not to panic. I'd seen Kevin at his worst—I figured he was just having a bad day. Frustration and anger at his injury were common. I understood he was suffering; it wasn't news to me. But Paul wasn't used to these outbursts, so he was terrified and wanted to intervene.

"I'll go check on him," I assured Paul, and hung up the phone.

Kevin and Lorena lived only five minutes from my house in Folsom, and I drove over without thinking much about it. I knocked on the door.

"Get the fuck out of here," Kevin yelled from the other side of the door.

What? A cold feeling of dread washed over me. Kevin never reacted to me in that way. Now I was scared.

"Kevin," I said his name warily from the outside stoop, so as not to upset him further. "Are you okay? What's going on?"

"Get the fuck out of here!"

I was so shocked at his language, and the rage in his voice, that now my panic, too, was escalating. *What was going on? Was he actually going to kill himself? Did he have a weapon? What was happening to him?* Twenty-five years of clinical training as a social worker, and all of that went right out the window at this moment. I backed away from the door.

Shaking, I got into my car and drove home to regroup. I'd had a meeting already scheduled with a family therapist, so, in desperation, I called him for help, but all he did was dismiss me, causing my panic to rise. My brain had gone offline in my terror, and my fight-or-flight response was now fully engaged. But I had to regain control, if not for me, at least for Kevin's sake. Finally, I pulled myself together enough to call the psychiatric hospital. The woman on the line was calm and reassuring.

"Call the police and have them do a wellness check," she advised.

The phone felt like it weighed a ton in my hand. *Call the police?* I had never called the police on a family member in my life. Wasn't that too extreme? What would they do? Would it push Kevin over the edge? Would it be one of those standoff situations where someone having a mental breakdown gets shot and killed because the police believe they have a weapon? Was I doing the right thing?

Terrified, I shakily dialed 911, and the responder remained calm and reassuring as well. She explained that all they would do was knock on the door, ask some questions, and see how he was doing.

The waiting left me paralyzed with fear. I kept checking the clock. Ten minutes went by. What was happening? Then another twenty. Have they gone over yet? I waited for another thirty minutes, but there was no call back. No information. Finally, I gave up waiting and made the decision to drive by Kevin's house. I sagged in relief when I saw the police car parked in front. I parked next door and walked over to the officers. One of them stopped me from proceeding to the house. I stopped, exasperated, and explained that I was his mother.

"Ma'am, he doesn't want you here. He said he would file a restraining order on you if you don't vacate the property."

I was gobsmacked. *A restraining order?* There had to be some kind of mistake. Did they know who I was? Clearly, they did not appreciate the gravity of the situation. "Look, I got a call that he was telling someone he was going to kill himself. I didn't make this up," I argued.

"I understand, but he's talking to us and he's fine. We know him. We see him around town, and he's fine, but you'll need to leave."

The officer stood there staring at me and his look said it all: I was the crazy one. Like I had been the one to invent the danger since Kevin was acting like his old, charming self. It was a kick in the gut; I was humiliated and furious. Didn't Kevin remember all those nights I had slept on a dirty hospital floor so he would feel secure? And now he was going to file a restraining order on me? What the hell! We had had no argument. My last conversation with him was fine. There had been no conflict between us. I was done. I was so fucking done sacrificing myself to help him. If no one else was on my side, if the police wouldn't believe me, if the therapists wouldn't believe me, if HE wouldn't believe me, what more could I do?

That afternoon I realized something so powerful it would take me weeks to process. I was alone in this fight. Kevin had walked over the line, turned around, and aimed straight at my heart. Because of his distorted world of false assumptions, he lashed out at both Paul and me. "Paul was disloyal," he would later assert. "And you didn't have my back."

That hurt. Didn't he see that I was the only one who did have his back? Yet even though his interpretation of events didn't match our experience at all, he couldn't process our fear. He couldn't understand how we—I—had lived through his brain injury. He couldn't understand the trauma and fear I lived with every day. He couldn't put himself in my shoes; he couldn't imagine my concern and terror.

I didn't talk to Kevin for a few weeks after that. I couldn't. I may have understood cognitively that his anger and response were all related to his brain injury, but the hurt was too fresh, too raw. Eventually, though, Kevin started to talk to me as if nothing had happened. I knew that he dealt with short-term memory loss—maybe he didn't recall all the facts? Still, I couldn't deny it damaged our relationship for a while. Kevin might not have remembered everything that had happened, but I did. And as much as I often pushed aside my own feelings for the sake of my children, I couldn't easily dismiss them now.

But for all the tension the incident caused between Kevin and me, I didn't regret a single thing about my actions—or Paul's, too, for that matter. Despite the fact that Kevin was left with the belief that Paul and I had been disloyal to him, I wouldn't have changed what we did.

"It was wrong," Paul would tell me, regretting what he felt had been an overreaction.

"No," I insisted. "You had to speak up. You always have to tell someone if you think a person is suicidal. You don't take on that responsibility yourself."

If anything, Paul's deep concern and my own proved we were the opposite of disloyal. We didn't know what was going on, and I would never actually find out, but despite the fallout I'm confident I made the right decision to get involved.

I wanted to be angry with Kevin, too, like I would be if anyone else had done such an irrational thing to me. But whatever residual anger I had eventually gave way to pain because I knew it wasn't really Kevin; it was the damage to his brain that created this imposter. And in that, came a resurging realization that broke the pieces of my heart into tiny, tiny little fragments all over again. Kevin was truly gone.

Ultimately, what I would come to appreciate much later was that my grief at losing my son started long before his death.

CHAPTER 20

Turning Point

As Kevin and Lorena grew closer during their marriage, they felt settled enough to have a baby. Once they decided to have a child, Lorena got pregnant right away. She wrote a message to Kevin on a baseball and a onesie, announcing her pregnancy. He was over the moon—they both were. Though Carmen and Ozzie were not his biological children, Kevin couldn't have loved them more; now there would be one more child to love.

As Lorena's pregnancy progressed, I became privy to privileged information; I knew the sex of the baby from being at the doctor's visit during the ultrasound, but both Kevin and Lorena chose not to know the sex until the gender reveal. They were ecstatic when, during the party, they shot off a little cannon with the color blue. Lorena knew that Kevin would enjoy having a son.

When Lorena's mother came to visit, it proved to be the turning point in their love story.

Lorena did not have permanent resident status when she met Kevin. Her new marital status changed that position and even allowed her to go back to Mexico to visit her family after a nearly ten-year absence. Over time, some of her family received visas to visit her in the US; one of the first people to visit was her mother.

Lorena's mother was different. She had little to no education; her life had been spent raising her children and taking care of her home. Her house had dirt floors and inadequate bathroom facilities. Her life was hard, and I always got a sense that she harbored resentment because of it. It took me a while to put my finger on it, but Lorena's mother was incredibly insular, and her acceptance did not include Kevin. Rather, it made him a punching bag for years of anger that had been repressed. Lorena had left Mexico at a young age, and I think that caused her to miss out on her connection to her mother, and in an attempt to bond with her, Lorena chose to side with her on every issue. It was like they had decided to form an alliance against Kevin. Whether it was not getting dinner on the table in time or pointing out his inability to multitask, Kevin became the object of their scrutiny. And yet, with all the focus they put on Kevin, they completely missed the fact that he had special needs because his brain was different.

Kevin needed quiet, he needed calm, he needed the space to complete one task at a time. But beyond those day-to-day annoyances, what really disturbed Kevin was this feeling that Lorena was loyal to her mother, above all else. When he would vent about feeling on the outside, I would try to explain that just as Lorena couldn't see or understand Kevin's lingering trauma from his accident, so, too, he couldn't see the lingering trauma from her childhood. She'd missed out on her mother's love all those years; she was searching for it now that her mother was back in her life. Kevin said he understood, but it still left him feeling hurt and confused; it made more sense to him that her mother should have been grateful to Kevin for helping Lorena get resident status so she could see her family again. It had opened many doors for her, yet all he seemed to do was trigger hostile feelings in her. Tension between Kevin and Lorena grew; his marriage was now hanging by a thread. The sweet little family unit they shared seemed to be dangling dangerously.

Kevin was completely bewildered by this turn of events. As with many marriages, he didn't feel that this was what he had bargained for. Between Lorena's mother and the multiple family members that would come and stay, we, too, lost Lorena.

There was an overwhelming feeling of resentment toward Kevin for not being a good enough provider. Kevin brought in a little income from disability, and so Lorena didn't have to support him. But as time progressed it became clear that this was not the marriage she had been expecting either. Lorena brought in an income through cleaning houses, and since Kevin "stayed at home," he took on the bulk of the childcare and volunteer duties. He was the one who attended the teacher conferences and coached the basketball teams. "You may be a good father," she would tell him, "but you're not a good husband." To her, a high-paying job was the standard measurement of a successful marriage.

The barrier to the life Lorena had pictured with Kevin was always going to be that she didn't understand just how truly impaired he was. She couldn't see his limitations, therefore, they didn't exist. Instead of hearing me out, or listening to Kevin's explanations, she would dismiss us with a wave. "Oh, he's fine," she'd often say.

But Kevin kept striving for that "normal" and did his best to show Lorena that he was capable of being a good husband. Given his experience estimating client costs in John's roofing company, he was able to offer Lorena ideas on exactly how to do an estimate for a new customer and set up her business in a more professional way. Instead of considering this teamwork, Lorena collected this as evidence that Kevin could work; he was simply choosing not to.

Kevin tried to educate her; he invited her to join him at one of his neurologist appointments. She went once, but never returned. "I didn't like the doctor," she said.

The strong pain medication Kevin was taking also became an issue between them, and I felt for them both. Kevin was on a dangerous roller coaster: getting his pain medication, using more than prescribed, running out, then going through withdrawal until his next prescription could be filled. For Lorena, it was a roller coaster she couldn't handle— to be fair, none of us could. What hurt me, though, was the way she chose to deal with it.

Lorena would treat Kevin with disdain, put him down, ridicule him, reject him, not talk to him, ice him out. At times, by her own admission, she was cold and cruel. It took me a very long time to heal from the pain this caused, but eventually, I was able to move outside of my own pain and see things from Lorena's perspective. Once I was able to do that, I could forgive her and start fresh in our relationship.

It was Christmas 2017 and we were still a few weeks away from the birth of Kevin's first child, and Lorena, moody in her late-stage pregnancy, was angry at Kevin. She was worried about many things with a child on the way, particularly how she would manage a baby and a business. The pain medication was also a concern. Kevin was trying to manage his pain; he was working with his doctors constantly, but Lorena couldn't seem to see the difference between Kevin doing his level best to manage his pain and a street drug addict. She couldn't understand that Kevin needed the drugs to have any kind of quality of life.

On Christmas Eve, as was her tradition, Lorena went to spend the evening with her aunts and cousins who lived about half an hour away. Normally, Kevin joined her, but this time she told Kevin he wasn't welcome with her family. Hurt and despairing, he didn't know how to make her happy, no matter how hard he tried. But beneath the hurt, there was also relief. He could hardly deal with loud parties, and there would be drinking, which he did not want to participate in. Instead, he waited up for Lorena, Carmen, and Ozzie to get home. They had planned to gather around the tree to open gifts at midnight. Kevin had been looking forward to the moment for a long time because he had been saving to get each of them the perfect gift. Regardless of what he chose, he always put a lot of thought into the gifts he picked for each person. That year had been no exception.

As the clock grew closer to midnight, Kevin fell asleep. When Lorena and the kids got home, Lorena didn't want to wake him because she was angry. Lorena was trying to teach Kevin a lesson, that using pain medication meant no marriage to her. So they opened all their gifts without him.

When Kevin woke the next morning, he was crushed.

What breaks my heart—and what, of course, we didn't know then—was that would be Kevin's last Christmas. Never again would he be able to witness Carmen and Ozzie open their gifts. Never again would he be able to choose the perfect gift for the kids. Never again would he experience the children's joy of Christmas.

Christmas Day for all of us had also been ruined. Instead of Kevin's whole family coming to our house for dinner and gifts, only Kevin arrived. A while later, Carmen insisted she wanted to come, so Lorena dropped her and Ozzie off at our house. I had to work really hard to rein in my own temper; I believed that adults, no matter their issues, should do their best to hold it together for family time, especially the holidays. But instead, Lorena's frustration with Kevin spilled over into Christmas.

I was angry with her for a long time, especially in the months to follow. But after Kevin died, my animosity faded. It had to, because ultimately, I love Lorena; I always have, despite my own frustrations.

We were both suffering; we'd both experienced the trauma that involves losing a person we loved. And Kevin's death would become our bond.

After the Christmas incident, Lorena's anger intensified when her mother arrived while they waited for the baby to come. The night Lorena went into labor, she instructed Kevin to take a shower, so he jumped in to get ready for the hospital. Minutes later, she was banging on the door.

"I need to go now!" Her contractions were coming on swift, and as this was her third baby, she knew time was of the essence.

Kevin hurried out of the shower as Lorena's mother threatened to pull him out. Lorena called me.

"Kevin won't take me to the hospital because he's in the shower!"

I gasped, not understanding in the least. "I'll be right over."

By the time I got there, Lorena had already left with her mother. Kevin was, yet again, baffled. "Is this how pregnant women act?"

I shook my head.

"I was only in the shower for a few minutes; I was rinsing off the soap as fast as I could. What's going on with her?"

"I don't know," I replied. "But, get in the car, I'm taking you to the hospital."

Kevin and I arrived minutes after Lorena. She was asking to be admitted immediately, but there wasn't any emergency, so the staff took their time. Lorena had just been anxious. She was stressed and overwhelmed. All those emotions needed to land somewhere, and Kevin was always the closest. Kevin let out a slow breath. Whatever her mood, whatever her reasons, he was here with her now, readying for the birth of their son.

Labor went smoothly, and when Mikey was born, the room erupted in joy. Despite the anger, frustration, and sides that seemed to have been drawn in Kevin's household, the baby brought them back together. Both Kevin and Lorena were overjoyed and they fell in love with their sweet baby boy instantly.

In the moments after he was born, it felt like this beautiful baby had brought us all together to heal. Lorena asked Kevin to name him, and after some careful consideration, he chose Mike, after his grandfather, my dad, who was a real inspiration to him. He gave Mike the middle name of James so he would have the initials MJ after Michael Jordan, his favorite basketball player. The nickname, Mikey, however, picked up quickly. This small bundle was a gift. Now Carmen, Ozzie, Lorena, and Kevin were all bound by blood, connected through Mikey. It solidified the family. That night, there was so much love, joy, and hope.

"I can't believe you are mine. I can't believe you are mine." I nearly wept as I watched Kevin hold his son.

CHAPTER 21

CPS

"Kevin killed the baby! Kevin killed the baby!" Carmen called me, frantic, hysterical, crying, and shouting.

I couldn't get anything more out of the thirteen-year-old girl, so, in a complete panic, John and I rushed over to their house, my mind conjuring the worst-case scenarios. *What could possibly have happened?* Five minutes later, I flew through the door and grabbed the three-month-old baby from Lorena.

He was fine. Awake. Alert. Breathing. Making eye contact with me. *What the hell happened?*

The police showed up; the officer took Mikey from me, laid him on a chair and examined him. He was as perplexed as I was. "Is this her first baby?" he asked John and me.

"No," we both replied in confusion.

None of us could understand what had gone on, but as a precaution, the police called an ambulance to transport Mikey to the hospital since they couldn't make any medical decisions. They kept Mikey overnight for observation.

I stayed at the hospital all night. Mikey was fine; he had a little cold, that was all, but I wanted to see for myself. I didn't fully trust Lorena at this point, especially after this disturbing display. Why would she have accused Kevin of killing the baby? It made no sense.

As the night went on, I had learned that Kevin hadn't even been alone with the baby. Lorena had taken Mikey to the mall with Carmen and Ozzie; they'd been gone most of the day. When they got home, Kevin had taken the baby to calm him because he was crying. When Mikey was circumcised, Kevin had seen the nurse dip her finger in sugar water to soothe him, so that night, when Mikey got fussy, Kevin had dipped a tiny bit of honey on his finger and let Mikey suck on it. Lorena's account was that a few hours later, Mikey was staring at the ceiling and unresponsive, causing her to become hysterical. She'd read online that it was unsafe to give honey to a baby under one year— honey in large amounts could potentially cause botulism—so in her agitated state, she had determined Kevin had killed the baby. She freaked Carmen out, too, who then called me.

It was all a colossal misunderstanding that would have incredibly grave repercussions for all of us. Based on Lorena's accusations, the hospital had no choice but to contact Child Protective Services (CPS), who then interviewed Kevin, who was, by then, a mess. With his brain injury, he could hardly process what was happening. His anxiety made him unable to think or talk clearly, so he was told by CPS he needed to move out of his home while the incident was being investigated.

Kevin was stunned. He hadn't even been holding the baby when the incident happened. The amount of honey he'd given to Mikey was miniscule at best; Mikey had never been in any danger. In fact, later, Lorena sheepishly admitted to me that the doctor thought she had completely overreacted. The diagnosis was a simple stuffy nose. No assault. No danger.

But CPS did not drop their investigation. The CPS worker interviewed Lorena, Carmen, and Ozzie, and despite all evidence to the contrary, Lorena requested that Kevin only get visitation with Mikey if I was there to supervise. CPS called me to see if I would agree to the visitation request of four hours a day supervising Kevin with the baby. Of course I agreed because it was the only way Kevin would get time with his son, but still, I was baffled.

"Why is this order even in place since the pediatrician has ruled out everything but a stuffy nose?"

"We have . . . concerns . . ." She went on to explain that Lorena had described Kevin as an irresponsible father addicted to drugs who couldn't care for a baby.

"Are you kidding?" I seethed. How could CPS make decisions based only on one parent's account of the situation? The only contact made with Kevin was to communicate that he had to vacate the house before Mikey came home. The repeated injustices shattered me.

"We'll make an appointment to come to your house to interview Kevin," the CPS worker conceded after I continued to lobby for my son.

It was no surprise that during the interview, Kevin was alert, present, and could answer all the questions intelligently and calmly. "He isn't anything like his wife described," the caseworker said to me afterward.

Again, I could feel my anger flare up as I made the observation that Kevin was still separated from his son. "We have to finish our investigation," she answered flatly.

That was all. We have to finish our investigation.

As much as I may have made peace with Lorena and her mother after Mikey was born, old resentments began to seep into the fragmented pieces of my heart and imbed themselves in my mind. We were caught up in a giant tug of war over control, and Mikey was going to pay the ultimate price. Kevin was heartbroken. He'd done everything he could, and still it wasn't enough. He'd started on Suboxone to wean off his pain medication—which is something they both wanted.

Kevin was tired of the cycle of pain: medication, overuse, and withdrawal. He didn't want this to continue impacting his family life, but though Suboxone was supposed to provide some pain relief, for Kevin it turned out to be a terrible medication with horrendous side effects. Kevin was talking rapidly and didn't make sense at times. I couldn't understand what was happening to him.

I took him to the emergency room, where the evaluating doctor surprised me with a question. "You're a licensed clinical social worker. What are your thoughts? Do you think he needs to be in a psychiatric hospital?"

I stared at him, dumbfounded. "How can I make that decision? I'm his mother." I was much too emotionally involved to make an objective decision. All I wanted was to get the best care for Kevin. Ideally, I wanted to take him back home with me, but the last few days had grown intense. Kevin hadn't been himself. I needed him to be observed and given an outside evaluation. But when the doctor asked me what I thought about the whole situation, I realized the sad truth: I was beginning to be the expert on Kevin's TBI and medication. By this point, I had more hands-on experience dealing with a brain injury than most doctors because I had learned "on the job."

Finally, the doctor decided to admit Kevin to a psychiatric hospital for evaluation. Kevin was not happy. Upon his release two days later, the determination was that he had had a reaction to the Suboxone due to his brain injury, and he was advised to never take it again.

The whole experience had been jarring for all of us; it was frightening for Kevin to be around patients with severe mental illness in full-blown psychosis, and thankfully, the doctor quickly realized Kevin wasn't having a psychotic episode, but still Kevin was frustrated. Everything he tried to help him get off the pain medicines provided no relief. Everybody had an answer. But none of those answers solved the problem.

As always, I was working tirelessly to get my son the help he needed. What was frustrating was that I was never actually sure what that help was supposed to look like. I may have been in the mental health field, but that didn't mean I had any expertise in long-lasting impacts from traumatic brain injuries—and addictions. There were physical, medical pieces to the puzzle that I was profoundly unqualified for, yet still, it was up to me. I was tired too. As tired as Kevin, though by no means would I have compared our plights. Still, it was agonizing to watch Kevin falter and to know his own family was at stake too.

Finally, I came across a PhD psychotherapist an hour away who specialized in traumatic brain injuries and addiction. I set up an appointment immediately. When we met with the psychotherapist, she explained that Kevin's brain chemistry had been altered by the injury, and it wasn't uncommon for TBI patients to have a reaction to medications like Suboxone.

I heaved a sigh. I wasn't sure if it was relief that we were finally getting some answers, or frustration that none of the other medical professionals seemed to have known that. How much better off would Kevin have been from the start if we'd all had more information?

"I'd try another method of pain relief if I were you," she told Kevin.

I laughed. As if it were that simple. "Like what?"

"CBD." CBD, the short form for cannabidiol, is a component of medical marijuana. "Some TBI patients find that CBD gives them more relief than the pain medication without the side effects of addiction."

He hurried back to his pain management doctor, his hope riding high.

"No," she said emphatically, discouraging the medical marijuana idea. "It's simply another drug. And, it's not a good idea to stop all pain medication. Your injury causes you debilitating pain, so you need to stay on the pain medication."

Kevin heard her. But he also couldn't ignore Lorena's ultimatum; if he didn't get off the medications, he could lose his whole family, newborn baby included.

"No more," he told his doctor. "Don't give me anymore."

She put that in his chart: he was requesting not to be prescribed any more pain medication.

It took CPS six months to complete their investigation. They concluded nothing had happened and that there was absolutely no foundation to the claims Lorena had made about Kevin and Mikey.

Yet still, the whole ordeal had left me feeling like a spinning top, as if someone had come down from heaven, pushed my head, and left me on my own, to spin and spin and spin until I ran out of inertia. I felt sick, scared, and stressed. It was painful to watch Kevin fall further into suffering. I knew I was too close to the situation to see things clearly; I couldn't even figure out what to think or believe.

Though Kevin was cleared, it came as no surprise that he and Lorena separated as a result of the CPS fiasco. Lorena insisted Kevin be the one to file for divorce even though Kevin didn't want a divorce. He still loved her and their kids.

Ultimately, Kevin was forced to file to get child custody issues resolved. The situation with Mikey was growing more difficult, and I wanted to make sure Kevin and his parental rights were respected.

"Go see an attorney," I urged. "Get child custody arranged legally."

What I didn't tell Kevin—though I'm sure he knew—was that Lorena wouldn't be able to use Mikey against him if the custody matters were decided in court.

There was very little I could do. We'd given Kevin a place to stay, we'd loaned him money for his legal proceedings, and I continued to search for new ways to help him, but the hard fact was that without proper pain medication, Kevin could barely function. He could hardly get out of bed as his headaches sucked the life out of him. On the days he had Mikey and couldn't function, I would step in. I loved helping with Mikey, and it was yet another way for the two of us to bond over his own baby. I helped Kevin develop a routine for play time, feeding, and taking Mikey for walks, and those routines helped Kevin too. It was the little things, like playing Bob Marley to put Mikey to sleep, that showed just how sweet of a relationship Kevin had with his son.

"I can't believe you're mine," he'd whisper as he rocked him to sleep to the soft sounds of "This is Love."

And still, Kevin held out hope he could win his family back. In the meantime, he wanted to be the best version of himself for Mikey. He dove into his efforts to seek alternative methods of dealing with the pain. Together we explored every option; we left no stone unturned.

We investigated a treatment program for opioid addiction which offered alternative pain treatments. It was expensive but, though John and I didn't have tons of money, we were willing to pay out of pocket. We were willing to do anything to help Kevin even if it meant tapping into our savings. What we couldn't help with was the waiting list—it was nine months long. *Nine months?* Kevin needed help now. He wanted to try acupuncture, the best acupuncture doctor in town who dealt with these issues had a waiting list about a year long. We kept running up against roadblocks. We found a doctor who practiced cranial sacral therapy, a specialized form of a gentle, hands-on massage for the head, neck, and back, and for which I paid out of pocket, but it also didn't provide much relief. Kevin had been seeing a chiropractor for years, and though he believed it helped, he couldn't afford the two-to-three-times-a-week visits he would have needed.

Eventually we did try CBD—an acquaintance of mine made edibles with CBD, so I arranged for a tincture which she promised would provide pain relief. We met in a parking lot to exchange money for the tincture—it felt so sleazy, but I was willing to try anything. Since there isn't a standardized dose, Kevin used too much and began to hallucinate. His friend called me, advising me to get him orange juice to bring down the high. It helped bring him back down, but we realized the amount he needed to get the relief from pain he was seeking was not a dose that he could sustain and still take care of Mikey.

In my research, I discovered methadone as a possible solution, something I hadn't considered before. I thought this might finally be perfect. Pain relief that was managed and regulated. It would require Kevin to go in every day for several months to take his methadone, under the supervision of medical staff. After a stabilization period, Kevin would then be able to take the methadone at home. The program also required individual and group counseling. This seemed to be the answer. As we walked into the methadone clinic, Kevin was greeted by other clients who supported and encouraged him. We were so hopeful. But after a brief conversation to evaluate Kevin for the program, the staff told us he was not a candidate for the methadone program because he had a chronic pain problem. They believed the methadone would not fully relieve his pain which would force him into drug-seeking behavior outside of the program. They couldn't take that risk with him.

The irony. If Kevin had been "just an addict," then he could have gotten help. But because he had a legitimate need for the pain medication, one that saw him get addicted, he couldn't get help.

We were so disappointed. It had been our last-ditch effort to get both the pain relief he needed and to manage the addiction. When we drove off, my stomach clenched in agony. It felt like the last nail in the coffin. We had run out of alternatives. There was no answer to the chronic pain. If he was to have any life at all, he would have to go back on his pain medication and that was that. But given Lorena's insistent demands about Kevin's drug use, he feared the possibility of never being with his family again.

It was a dark day.

I felt every stab of his suffering. It was agonizing to see him rejected and heartbroken, and despite all my efforts, I couldn't fix it. I couldn't protect him.

I was angry at the medical profession for not fixing him, angry at Lorena for rejecting him, angry at myself for failing him. I needed someone to blame. Blame, I would learn later, creates an illusion of control, an illusion that this situation could be fixed if only. If only the doctors had a solution, a medication, a treatment. If only they hadn't given him oxycodone in the first place. If only Lorena could have been kind and supportive, if only she could have shown more compassion.

I didn't absolve myself either. I was guilty. Somehow, this was my fault. If only I had done something different. What did I fail to do that made it all go so wrong? What could I have changed to prevent the brain injury in the first place? Kevin's drinking? His nights out? *Hindsight bias* is what they call it, where you look back with the information you have in the present to try to explain the past.

But there was no solution. There was nowhere to turn. Sadness, guilt, grief, powerlessness; it all mixed together inside of me and formed a powerful cocktail of emotion. I desperately longed for something to take away all the pain for Kevin, for myself, for my family.

What I did not count on was trading one form of pain for something much, much worse.

CHAPTER 22

The End

Kevin had been off pain medication for six months. Despite the horrific pain he experienced every day, he'd managed to resist reaching for drugs. He'd been trying so hard to win his family back, though it didn't seem to be working very quickly, and the pressures were taking their toll. The loss of his family, the pain of the CPS-enforced separation from Mikey, and the ongoing battle for his self-worth were overwhelming.

"I can't even afford to buy him a toy," Kevin told me, as his frustration over not being able to hold down a job took over our conversation about his baby boy.

"We'll always help you," I reassured him.

But that wasn't what he wanted. Kevin wanted to be a provider, and because he couldn't be one in the traditional sense of the word, he felt like a failure as a father and a husband.

It broke my heart.

I was always worried about him, but my anxiety over his condition had ramped up recently. Only a few days earlier, I'd been standing in the hallway when Kevin walked out of his room. Immediately, I gasped.

"Kevin, something's wrong. You have such dark circles under your eyes." My voice cracked as my fear rose. I started to cry.

"Oh, Mom," he replied, with such utter resignation and despair, "I'm just not getting enough sleep from the head injury. I'm in so much pain."

The pain, almost intolerable without medication, kept him from sleeping at night, so he was forced to try to sleep when he could. Sometimes he would finally fall asleep at four or five in the morning and sleep until the afternoon, though there was no regular pattern. Like searching out alternatives for the pain medication, Kevin tried everything to fall asleep. White noise machines, meditation, eye masks, lavender oil, exercise. Nothing worked, not even the strongest sleep medications.

Inside, I was panicking. I knew something was wrong, but I also knew deep down I couldn't fix all these problems for him. I wanted to, badly. He didn't deserve this. Later I would learn the symptoms I was witnessing, the dark circles, enlarged belly and fatigue, were indications of an enlarged heart, a condition where the heart increases in size and has to work harder. Sadly this was due to damage to his heart—either from the stress, the drug use and withdrawal, or just an inherited condition. Yet, we all knew Kevin's heart was large indeed; he always had a big heart full of love and compassion.

I started having dreams that I found him dead. In one dream, I found Kevin lying on his bed in his room with no signs of life and called Lorena. *"Kevin's dead! Kevin's dead! You got what you wanted! You got it all!"* In my dream, Lorena wanted the house, cars, money, and the kids. I thought my dream was about my anger at her behavior. I didn't realize, until it was too late, that it had been a premonition.

I couldn't have known that soon, in my own waking nightmare, I would say to her a variation of those very words. Kevin's dead. Kevin's dead.

Kevin was still living with us. It had been six months, and to my knowledge, he had been sober for those six months. I hate using the word *sober* to describe it, since it's meant to sound like a victory, but in reality, Kevin had been in debilitating pain without his much-needed pain medication for six months. There was no victory in that.

I needed help taking Danny's car to get a tire replaced, and Kevin agreed to help me. On the way, Kevin and I stopped at our old house. Two weeks earlier, we'd moved into our brand new, built-from-the-ground-up dream home, and though it was exciting, the move had also been stressful. We still had a few chores to take care of in the old house before we put it on the market, and, as usual, Kevin jumped in to help without asking. He'd always been attuned to what needed to be done; if he saw a need, he simply took care of it. In this case, it was vacuuming. He saw the upstairs needed vacuuming, so he did it. I remember thanking him, feeling so appreciative that he'd lightened my load.

As we drove out of the driveway, off to the tire store, Kevin and I talked about some of the stress going on in my life and in his.

"This move has you too stressed, Mom," he said. "It's having an impact on you."

Kevin wasn't blind; he knew my stress also had to do with his own situation; he could always tap into the connection we shared and tell me accurately what he saw. But his comment that day stung especially because a few days earlier he and I had had a fight. We didn't usually argue, but I'd been angry with him for not helping more with the move. He had made himself scarce—not his normal helpful self, the guy I could always depend on for taking care of daily chores.

I had asked him to show up at the new house to wait for thirty minutes for someone to come and hook something up, and I just assumed he would be available—what else did he have to do? Given how much I'd helped him take care of his son every day for six months, I figured it was the least he could do. But Kevin had a hard time with the move. Our old house had been only a few blocks from Lorena and the kids; moving fifteen minutes away to a new neighborhood felt like a loss to him, so when I'd asked for the favor, he'd blown up at me.

"You are the ones who wanted to move. It's not my job to take care of your move!"

Are you kidding me? We were providing a home for him to live in, food to eat most of the time, and we paid for his lawyer for the divorce. What was thirty minutes of his time to help me out? What I couldn't see, until later, was that his reaction had nothing to do with helping or not helping me. It had everything to do with Kevin feeling overwhelmed. He didn't want a divorce, and moving to another location made him feel not just physically further from Mikey, but also emotionally. The move was disruptive to him. But in the heat of the moment, when he'd raised his voice to me, I had felt threatened.

"You're a big man," I warned him. "When you raise your voice, it feels threatening to me as a woman." I was sharp in my reprimand, but I wasn't actually worried about him hurting me. Still, we exchanged harsh words.

In retrospect, I wish we'd have let it go. Tensions were running high over the move; we both knew that, yet we'd argued regardless. In the big picture, we shouldn't have wasted our words; it seems so ridiculously unimportant now but in the moment, the anger felt all too encompassing. It would be another action I'd have to learn to forgive myself for. Guilt and the grieving brain. The what-ifs and if onlys. If only I hadn't fought with him in our last few days together. What if I'd better understood his own frustration? It took time and effort and a better understanding of my body and brain's own reaction to grief to remind myself that all relationships experience conflicts, that no matter the love, tensions can boil over. Life can't be perfect, even if we want it to be, just on the off chance that something unexpected and tragic may happen to our loved ones. Would I have wished for a harmonious last few days with my son? Obviously. But if I'm wishing, I would wish that he'd never died in the first place.

I steered the conversation away from me and my stress as I drove to the tire store. "Kevin, you need to enjoy your life. Sometimes people with head injuries die unexpectedly."

Prescience.

I hadn't known, not really. If I had, I would have moved heaven and earth to stop Kevin's death, but the memory is haunting nonetheless.

"It happened to a former client of mine who had a head injury," I kept talking. "You don't know what the future holds, so enjoy your life."

You don't know what the future holds.

You don't know that tomorrow at this time, your beloved son will be dead.

You don't know that you will never be whole again.

Kevin just looked at me. He didn't say a word.

When we got to Big O Tires, Kevin waited with the car while I went inside. There were a few men in the waiting area, and one man was helping me with the paperwork. It was quiet as a graveyard; no one was saying a word. Then, Kevin walked in. Pretty soon I heard all this laughing and talking from the men who had just been silent. Kevin had started asking them about the sports game that was on the TV. Even with his brain injury, he was bringing the room to life with his light. He'd always been like that. He was always the life of the party. He was always the one who got everyone involved, whether it was a room full of relatives or strangers in a sports bar or tire shop, Kevin had that rare quality I have always envied—he could put anyone at ease.

As I completed the paperwork, I couldn't help but smile.

Later, I would look back on Kevin's last day in microscopic inspection. Always the what-ifs and if onlys, but also the small moments, the warm moments. Kevin helping me at the old house without asking; Kevin's spark of camaraderie with the others in that store. Kevin being

Kevin. On Kevin's last day, Kevin—not his brain injury, or his pain, or his losses and stress and challenges—shone through. Kevin was exactly how he was created to be.

To this day, I cling to that.

We left the tire store and stopped for pizza at Dominic's, his favorite where he was a regular. The owner, Dominic, loved Kevin, too, in part because Kevin always showed an interest in Dominic's business. In spite of all his difficulties, Kevin always rooted for others' success. He could have turned inward; he could have become bitter. He could have looked around and seen so many other people living "better," more successful lives, but despite Kevin's despair at his own situation, he never begrudged another soul for their own happiness. He just wanted his share too.

For some reason, Kevin looked better that day. Earlier in the morning, he had gone to the gym to work out, something he loved. It was one of the things he could still enjoy doing. Maybe it helped his stress and made him feel better, I didn't know, but regardless, I was glad to see him going to the gym. I had been surprised, since he had gone early that morning, which was unusual, given he mostly slept late unless he had Mikey, but like most things that day, I didn't question it.

No matter how much I might wish for a storybook script of Kevin's final day, there was still conflict. In the afternoon, Kevin had yet again pleaded with John to give him his job back.

"You have to hire me back," he implored.

I knew where he was coming from; he desperately wanted to work to make money and provide for his family, knowing the way Lorena valued work. He believed he could win her back if only he could work again. But both John and I knew it would be a disaster. Sure, Kevin could work for a day, but that would lead to mental fatigue for the rest of the week. It wouldn't have been sustainable, and we all knew it.

"No," John told him, feeling sad he couldn't help him..

"You'll lose your disability and healthcare," I reminded Kevin. "You know how difficult it would be to get back on disability if you returned to work." Though his actual disability check wasn't huge, the fact that his very high healthcare expenses were covered made the decision easy.

Still, Kevin made John the target of his frustration, and that led to even more tension in our house.

I pulled Kevin aside. "You cannot work for John," I reiterated.

"It's because John doesn't like me," Kevin complained. It was the furthest thing from the truth, but Kevin had gotten it into his head that John was the one who'd decided Kevin was unable to work— not the plethora of doctors and insurance people who could see he wasn't capable.

I took a deep breath. I understood there was more going on, a deeper layer to Kevin's anger. There was hurt and misplaced betrayal. "You've had issues with your biological father rejecting you because he was never in your life," I gently explained. "But now you're putting all that anger on John. John loves you. He's done more for you than any man in your life, you know that. He's the one who got you on disability with that letter he wrote. He's the one who's been trying to help you all this time. He's not against you. It wasn't him. You were tested by the Department of Vocational Rehabilitation—they were the ones who decided you could not return to work." I was on a roll. I couldn't stop. I was tired, so tired of being caught in the middle between my son and my husband. I understood Kevin's frustration with his limitations, and I could see why he felt he had to work, given Lorena's traditional belief that the man should be the main breadwinner, which weighed heavily on him—but I also felt for John. He'd done nothing but try to support Kevin all these years; he didn't deserve to take the brunt of Kevin's anger. "Stop blaming John for the fact that you cannot work. It's not because of John. You cannot work because of your head injury.

You need to accept that. Enjoy your life. Take care of Mikey. Work out at the gym. Live a simple life. That's okay. You're still worthy."

"Mom, I can't even afford to support my son. I feel like a loser."

You're still worthy. How could I get Kevin to believe me?

"Don't worry," I tried to reassure him. "We will help you. We will not abandon you. Just make taking care of Mikey the most important thing. You are a wonderful father. You are a better father than most men I know. Some of these 'super successful' fathers are not home with their children, yet you care for your baby. It's the most important job in the world to raise a child."

"Do you really mean that I am a good father or are you just saying that?"

"Yes, I do mean that," I answered unequivocally. "You are the best father I have ever seen. You have a gift."

Kevin deflated. He knew what I was saying was true—at least about his ability to work. He acknowledged that he'd had a lot of trouble focusing since his injury.

I just hoped he'd see the other parts of what I'd said were also true. He had worth as a stay-at-home dad. He was an incredible father. What he was doing was the most important thing for his child. Mikey was his lifeline; Mikey was the thread he was holding onto. He loved that little boy with all he had.

It wouldn't be enough.

On the last day of Kevin's life, he had been distressed all day because Lorena would not let him see Mikey. She had plans to go see her family thirty minutes away and was taking the baby with her. Kevin was crushed again, especially since Lorena was violating their custody arrangement.

Four days earlier, on the previous Tuesday, the court had granted Kevin more visitation, almost halftime. The judge indicated that the CPS report showed nothing had occurred. Calmer heads were finally prevailing, but still Lorena wouldn't let it go. She'd tried to use his head injury against him.

"But you knew he had a head injury before you decided to have a child," the judge rightly pointed out.

However, Lorena needed the illusion of control, so she took it into her mind that she was the one who had granted Kevin more custody, not the judge. Since Kevin was going to get their son more during the week, she took it upon herself to keep Mikey that weekend.

It was another blow to Kevin. Even later that evening, when she'd gotten home, she refused to let him have Mikey. She refused to even answer his call, another power play she used often. Later, after Kevin died, and as Lorena and I grew closer, she'd tell me she still lives with the guilt of her decision that day.

That day, Kevin shared his distress with me about Lorena using Mikey to hurt him—and her success with the tactic. He was heartbroken that another day had passed, and he hadn't gotten a chance to see his son. I tried to reframe it for him.

"It's okay to have a day off. You need the rest."

Kevin didn't agree. He couldn't feel restful without his son. In fact, he was restless.

Shortly after we talked about John, Kevin went into the TV room to say sorry in his own way, and to thank John for helping him out. I don't know exactly the words they exchanged, but they made amends with each other and were at peace with one another.

It might have been just another breather; tensions might have ratcheted up between them again in the future but given how the end was near—though none of us knew it—I would look back on that peace with a modicum of relief. Conflicts did exist in relationships. So, too, did closeness and connection. I was grateful that's how John and Kevin's story ended.

In the evening, Kevin, John, and I hung out together while they watched a baseball game. The Dodgers were playing. We ordered some Chinese food from Frank Fat's, one of our favorite places. Kevin offered to pick it up, and when he returned, he had twelve dollars in change. John told Kevin to keep it. It wasn't much, but it was one small way John was looking out for Kevin, making sure he had a little extra money for coffee or something.

After dinner, Kevin decided to go to the gym again.

"Again?" I asked, concerned, as I watched him lace up his Jordan's. "Didn't you already go to the gym this morning?" It was out of character for him to go twice in a day, but then again, the gym was his one escape.

"I like to work out. You said I should enjoy my life. I enjoy working out."

How could I argue? Though there was something in my gut that had me questioning him, because something didn't seem right, there was really nothing else to say. I reframed these doubts for myself. *Good, he's taking care of himself instead of sitting around feeling bad.*

But I was also looking forward to spending time with John. Any home move can be a lot of work, and I wanted to catch up with my husband. Given the stress that Kevin was going through and how it impacted us, I felt the deep need to reconnect with John. So, I have to admit that the last time I saw Kevin, I had actually been disappointed. When Kevin came home close to midnight, John had taken that as his cue to wrap up our chat. If I had known I'd never again talk to my son, if I had known that would be the last time I saw him alive, I would never have let a fleeting sense of disappointment cloud the moment. But we were all ignorant of what was to come.

Kevin got a glass of water, as my attention refocused on him. "Where have you been? You couldn't have been at the gym all these hours?"

"I was talking to Jordan."

This was a good thing. I knew there'd been tension between the two friends; they used to be so close—in fact, Jordan had been the one to insist his roommates call an ambulance after Kevin's accident, and I credit Jordan with saving Kevin's life. But they'd had a falling out over a misunderstanding, and when Kevin got sober and realized how his pain medication had affected his thinking about his friend, he'd called to apologize. Both of them were now on a new path, working toward spiritual growth. They'd reconnected, talking several times a day, for hours at a time. Jordan had helped Kevin so much in the past few months; Kevin had needed someone other than me to listen to him, especially about his feelings about Lorena, the kids, and the pending divorce. He would share with Jordan about his marriage counseling too. The week before, Lorena and Kevin had seen a therapist to discuss the mixed messages in their relationship. During that session, Lorena told the therapist she definitely wanted a divorce. The next week, the therapist advised Kevin to let go. She told him to find his own North Star. We all thought that might be a turning point, but then Kevin's hurt over Lorena withholding Mikey that day had spilled over, so he confided in Jordan. Jordan, who always and only had Kevin's best interest at heart, was furious with the way Lorena was treating him; he could see Kevin's vulnerability and struggle, and he tried to support Kevin as much as he could. It was a friendship for which I'll always be grateful. Though Kevin may have felt it at times, he was, in fact, not alone.

Still, Kevin's explanation that he'd sat out front of our new house in his car talking to Jordan for hours seemed suspicious. It was true we had poor phone reception in the house, but something felt off. I questioned him further, but he seemed open and honest. So yet again, I dismissed my gut feeling.

I'd have something else to learn to forgive myself for.

He talked to me of his friend's efforts to help a man who'd been sober for thirty-five years, but then went out and drank—and died. Kevin recognized his own vulnerabilities.

"Mom, I think I've had the disease since I was a kid."

"Yes," I replied, proud of his insight and his personal growth. We'd always worried about his drinking, and later, the legal drugs, but now he seemed to have a clearer picture of his own challenges. It gave me hope. Kevin was alive and well and—I believed—drug free. Here was the insightful Kevin I knew. He was making peace with the changes in his life.

"Well, good night," he said.

The last words I would ever hear my son speak.

"Good night," I replied.

The last words I would ever say to my son.

———

The next day, John and I spent hours cleaning in the garage. We had a dumpster for one more day, so we wanted to take advantage of having it on site. We began throwing away boxes of old papers and items we didn't need anymore. It was a purge of old stuff we'd brought from the previous home. John and I felt good that morning; we had accomplished so much.

By the time we left to run a few errands, we still hadn't seen Kevin. That wasn't unusual, given Kevin's irregular sleep pattern. But when we did stop to grab a sandwich, I thought of calling Kevin to ask if he wanted anything. I didn't though, figuring that despite the early afternoon hour, he was probably still asleep. Which, yes, was starting to grate on me. Kevin and I were supposed to get Mikey that day; it was late, and I needed to know the schedule.

When we got home, it was around a quarter to two, I knocked on his bedroom door, then opened it.

"Kevin, you need to—"

I froze. Kevin was on the bed, lifeless. His body was gray. His eyes, fixed in a dead stare.

The moment stretched, then contracted, an unreality morphing into a reality I could not comprehend. Then, suddenly, I burst out of the room, screaming. "Kevin's dead! Kevin's dead!"

It was like my dreams.

My nightmares.

Only now, I was awake, and this was real. *Oh god, how could this be real?*

I couldn't find my phone. I ran through the house looking for it. John rushed to Kevin's room, trying to shake him awake. He called 911. Danny had been outside, listening to music through his earbuds. He hadn't heard me scream, not even when I'd been calling his name. I grabbed him by the arm. He shrugged me off, looking at me with utter disdain for interrupting his music.

"Kevin's dead! Kevin's dead!" I shrieked. Danny looked at me, stunned for a moment, then flew from the backyard to the front door, then outside again, where he threw up.

I was hysterical. I couldn't think straight. I had my phone now, and I began calling people. Everyone had to know. Kevin was dead.

I called Lorena.

Like in my dreams.

"Kevin's dead! Kevin's dead!" I screamed into the phone. Unlike my dream, there was no malice so I did not tack on those hurtful words, *And you got what you wanted.*

I don't even remember her reaction.

I don't remember a lot from that day.

I called Kara next. "Kevin's dead! Kevin's dead!"

I don't know how many times I said those words that day.

Kara didn't believe me, though. She didn't want to. "Maybe he just took too much pain medication," she tried to reason.

She was wrong.

I called my sister Lori. "Kevin's dead! Kevin's dead!" I shouted into the phone.

"No, he's not," she insisted.

Why didn't anyone believe me?

"Never mind," I cried. "I'm going to call someone who will believe me."

As much as I so desperately wanted them all to be right, I was the one who had seen Kevin's body.

I knew dead when I saw it.

I called my sister Mimi. She wasn't available, so I spoke to my niece. "Tell her Kevin died."

"Okay," she replied. The first to believe me.

I called my niece Kim. I told her to tell my brother that Kevin died.

"I'll let him know," she said.

I didn't know what shattered me more. When the people I phoned didn't believe me or when they did.

Shock had set in, taking me down from hysterical to an unnatural calm. Slowly, I walked back to Kevin's room while we waited for the paramedics to arrive. The day itself is vague in my memory, some parts I recall, others I barely remember, but I had a crystal-clear thought as I made my way back down the dark hallway.

I can't fix this.

There is not one more doctor, one more treatment, one more medication. I couldn't fix this. It was over. I felt it down to my bone marrow.

Lorena drove up, crying hysterically, screaming, "NO! NO!"

Danny tried to comfort her. Kara and Matt arrived at the house with Jack. When the paramedics arrived, they grabbed Kevin off the bed and started working on him. *Why are they doing CPR? He's gray. He's obviously dead.*

Lorena started screaming at Kevin, putting the baby near him, begging for him to live. For some strange reason, I started yelling at Kevin too. I knew he was dead. Nobody had to tell me.

During this incredibly stressful, shocking time, I received a text: "We are not going to believe you. John said the paramedics heard something. So, we are not going to believe you." *What?*

As the paramedics wheeled him out, Lorena said to me as she put Mikey on her hip, "He's going to be okay." I was bewildered. Saying it didn't make it so. False hope was worse than no hope and I knew, to the depths of my soul, there was no hope.

Kara asked the paramedics if they had a heartbeat because they had a bag over him to breathe him.

"No."

"Did you ever have a heartbeat?"

"No. We are transporting him to the hospital to see what they can do."

We loaded into our cars.

"John, he's dead," I said, yet again. I knew, I knew, I knew. "They don't even have their siren on."

I called my aunt to tell her and asked her to pass it on to my cousin Stephanie, whom I couldn't immediately get a hold of. Stephanie was a rock for me—she had been with me through so much, showing me support and care. With the flurry of knee-jerk reactions against me and my news, I could have used that warmth and love in that moment. Instead, I texted my friend Nancy from my rosary group for prayers.

"Please pray for us. Kevin died today."

I don't know why I felt compelled to call so many people. The shock made me want to scream out to friends and family. It was my version of shouting it from the rooftop, I suppose. My entire world had just gone dark and I needed everyone to know it. It felt like I was trying to climb out of a deep hole to get some air, but I was buried and suffocating under the loss. Buried alive. Maybe I started telling people to make it real, because this was very much not real. Last night, Kevin had been alive. Fully alive. Now he was dead. My brain could not register the reality.

I would learn later that was my own mind protecting me from a pain so great I may not have survived it. I needed to be numb, to act without conscious or even emotional thought.

When we arrived at the hospital, I told the front desk my son had died and was being transported to their facility. They immediately ushered us into a room by ourselves. Stephanie arrived, and I fell into her warm embrace. I never told her what hospital we were being transported to but she figured it out. Her presence was soothing. I was grateful.

The doctor came into the room.

"I'm sorry," he stated compassionately. "Your son died today."

I stared at him blankly, and before I could think through what to say, I heard the words "I know. I could see he was dead" coming out of my mouth.

"Mother's intuition," he remarked wryly.

I shook my head. I may have been in shock, I may have not been thinking clearly, but I wasn't blind. "No, he was gray. He was dead. I don't know why the paramedics worked on him. Maybe they can't call his death in the field."

"No, they can call a death." No one ever explained why they chose to do CPR on a dead body. Maybe they saw our distress and wanted to appear they were going to help us. The doctor continued, "But you are right. He died in the early morning hours. He has been dead for hours. I suspect it was a drug interaction."

"But he's been off pain medication for six months," I stated emphatically, thinking about all the pain he had endured over the last months as a result of not taking them.

"It could just be his regular medications," the doctor explained. "They can interact and cause death."

"But he's been on them for years." I shook my head in disbelief. How? How could the medications he had been taking since his injury be the thing that would take him from us?

"It can happen after years of being on medications," was his only explanation, and then he stated again, "I'm sorry for your loss," his voice sympathetic and kind.

My mind was reeling. Drug interaction. How was that possible?

It would be months before we would learn the full picture. Months of speculation and heartache and questions until we got his autopsy results. Later, we'd learn that Kevin died from taking something that was a mixture of fentanyl and amphetamine, something like an over the counter drug like Sudafed, not an illegal substance like methamphetamine. We would also learn that unbeknownst to us, Kevin also had an enlarged heart. It was a trifecta of events contributing to his death. I would learn that Kevin had gone to the gym that night to buy some drugs to stop his pain. In no way had he expected the pill to be laced with fentanyl, though the fentanyl alone did not kill him. If any one of those had been missing—the fentanyl, amphetamine, or enlarged heart—he would still have been alive.

"You can go back and see him now," the doctor said softly, before turning to leave.

Lorena and Carmen arrived.

"Kevin died today," I said to them both blankly. "The doctor has confirmed it."

All of us went into the ER room to see Kevin. John, Lorena, Carmen, Mikey, Kara, Matt, Jack, Danny, and me. After John saw Kevin, he left to go get Ozzie to bring him to the hospital.

"He didn't make it," John tried to gently break the news to eleven-year-old Ozzie before they arrived at the hospital.

Ozzie burst into tears.

They had had a special relationship.

Carmen threw herself onto Kevin. Carmen was fourteen years old and she had known him since she was five; he was the only father she'd ever known.

"Wake up! Wake up!" Carmen wailed into his chest. It was the most real moment of the day. It was what I wanted to say but couldn't. It was what I wanted to do, but I was paralyzed. I felt I had to be strong for the children, so I made a conscious decision to hold it together. Kevin looked calm and peaceful. All the wrinkles and stress were gone from his face. He looked handsome even, and I bent down to kiss his forehead.

Oh my God. He was cold as ice.

Ice cold.

I couldn't stop shaking.

The priest from Kevin and Lorena's church arrived. He, too, was shocked at Kevin's sudden death. He had just seen him the day before at a baptism class, since Lorena and Kevin had planned to baptize Mikey in a few weeks. He prayed with us and blessed Kevin.

"This is the path for all of us," he said.

Yes, yes, of course, but like this? So suddenly? So unexpectedly?

We left the hospital, all of us devastated. It felt so empty and unreal, walking away, knowing Kevin wasn't following.

All four of my sisters decided to fly out. My friends brought over food. I was functioning, barely. I was a shell of myself. I might have appeared normal when I was talking to someone, but I wasn't there. I was between.

Between heaven and earth.

Between life and death.

———————————

With my sisters all coming out the next day, John and I had to get mattresses for two of the bedrooms. We were not prepared for guests since we had barely moved into our new house, but I had to function as if life was normal. I had to pick out new mattresses, sheets, blankets, and pillows. I was numb, in a state of shock. The world was moving on as if everything was fine and all I wanted to do was scream. *Don't you know someone who was so deeply loved died yesterday? My Kevin died. Stop the world! Stop moving! Stop laughing! Stop living!*

I moved through the day like a robot, like a machine that only resembles a human being, compartmentalizing my feelings to get tasks done. I had to make beds, put out towels, get soap, and shampoo. But my life had just radically changed. It was a seismic shift like the earth opening after an earthquake. I fell deeply into the crevice of loss.

My sisters arrived later that day. They offered me comfort and consolation. When I went back to the bedroom where I found Kevin dead, I tried searching for more clues. At that point, we still didn't know how he had died. I was desperate for answers. What had happened? Drug interaction, the doctor had said. It didn't make sense. I searched Kevin's belongings, but I found nothing but two dollars in his backpack.

He'd had twelve in change from our dinner order.

Where was the other ten dollars?

I started throwing around his backpack and kicking things on the floor, screaming, "What happened, Kevin? What the fuck happened? I don't know what happened. I don't want this! I don't want this!"

John came in, and with a sharp tone ordered me to stop. Like I had been acting ridiculous. I was stung by his attitude, but I would appreciate later that he could not handle the way I was showing my distress. In the moment, though, I didn't care. I'd just lost my son. I was allowed to be crazy. *What the fuck happened?*

My mind kept going back to the previous day. Twelve hours ago, he was still alive. Twenty-four hours ago, I was talking to him. He'd been so alive and now he was gone. It was impossible to comprehend. I've since learned it takes the brain years to grasp the death of a loved one especially in a sudden, tragic death. My heart was shattered. My brain was foggy. I couldn't concentrate. All I wanted to do was scream.

But reality continued to intrude. Sleeping arrangements concerned me. Who would want to sleep in Kevin's room where he had died? I could barely go back into the room myself. I did get a new mattress for the room because I thought it would be weird to have to sleep on a bed where somebody died twenty-four hours earlier. But when I went to the bedroom to discuss sleeping arrangements, I found Mimi already in the bed reading, and Lori was preparing to get in the bed too. I was so surprised that they hadn't hesitated to sleep in Kevin's room.

"How are you okay here?" I asked.

Mimi, whose husband had died of a sudden heart attack a few years before, answered. "I had to live in my house and go into my kitchen after Jim died. I'm not freaked out by being around a home where someone died. I do it every day."

Lori added her explanation. "I want to be here. This is where the angels came for him."

Wow. How beautiful. I had never thought of it that way. It was the scene of such an awful tragedy for me, yet Lori and Mimi helped me see it in a different light. For months, whenever I walked by that bedroom and images of Kevin dead on the bed would flood my mind, it helped to remember Lori's words.

This is where the angels came for him.

My brothers also came as soon as possible, and my father. Kevin and my father had a close bond. Kevin adored him—he'd named his son after him. They had loved to engage in sports talk together. They both religiously followed basketball, football, and baseball. They loved gambling on the games, discussing each play, predicting championship winners. Kevin and my dad also had deep man-to-man conversations about relationships with women. My father lost his dad at age thirteen to miner's consumption. He understood the pain of not having a father present. And though Kevin had met his biological father once, at the age of thirteen, it had been a dismal failure, and Kevin had never wanted to see him again. The hurt of his abandonment was too much. My dad understood, and he had become a father figure to Kevin. Their bond had always been solid.

Since my whole family had arrived, all nine brothers and sisters and some spouses, I realized it would be best to arrange the funeral that week, so they did not have to come back.

Kevin died on a Sunday. The priest was only available the following Friday, so that's when we arranged the funeral. The Rosary would be Thursday night.

Lorena, still officially his wife at the time of Kevin's death, planned his funeral with me, and I wanted her to. I knew people needed to participate in the funeral to feel connected to the one they lost. I also knew that, despite the divorce proceedings, Lorena still loved Kevin. Later, she would confide in me that she had always thought she and Kevin would reunite. It hadn't looked that way in the moment, and of course there's no telling what that alternate future would have been, but her comments were nonetheless reassuring that, despite her behavior she had indeed always loved Kevin.

The two of us went to the mortuary, but all the while I was thinking how surreal the whole scene was. We were planning a funeral for Kevin. It couldn't be so.

Kara and Danny both said they wanted to give a eulogy. The priest balked, arguing there could be only one eulogy, but I replied, "Kevin had two siblings. They both want to do eulogies." The priest relented.

Carmen and Ozzie would do readings, and I was so proud of their courage to participate and their desire to honor Kevin.

Lorena and I picked out a blue casket, since it was Kevin's favorite color, the color of North Carolina, his favorite basketball team. As we walked back to the car, she snapped at me. "We can't fight anymore."

My eyes widened. I had never been in a fight with her. As much as I hated how she had treated Kevin, I had always tried to be respectful of her during the separation. In retrospect, I could better see her issues of control as desperation; she was missing something fundamental from her life, her own childhood trauma rearing its head, and she'd taken it out on Kevin. Kevin, with his own issues, had been difficult to live with. They both brought complex, painful issues to their relationship. But as we stood in the parking lot of the funeral home, I pulled her into a hug. "We need each other," I said. Lorena might not have understood all the challenges and obstacles Kevin had faced because of his brain injury, and she may have acted cruelly to use their son against him, but regardless, she and I were the ones who understood Kevin's life better than anyone. We were bound together in grief, and that would create a relationship between the two of us that was built on care, compassion, and forgiveness.

Lorena and the kids decided to bury Kevin in Folsom where they lived so he would be close to them, and they opted not to cremate him, so Lorena and I picked out a plot together.

We asked Kevin's friends Jordan and Nick to be pallbearers. My brothers Steven and Paul were also pallbearers, as were Matt, Jack, and Ozzie.

So many people loved Kevin.

Thursday night we held the Rosary. In the Catholic Church, the Rosary, a devotion practice using a string of beads to count out and meditate on scripture-based prayers, is often prayed together the night before the funeral. The room was packed with all the people who had gathered. My friends Lou Ann and Nancy led the Rosary using our Rosary prayer book. Each bead has a specific meditation, and I was soothed by the beauty of the ritual.

Kevin lay in an open casket, the picture of perfect health, like he was sleeping. I couldn't help going over to the casket several times to stare at him; he looked perfectly fine.

Get up! I wanted to shout. *Your joke is over now!*

I wanted him raised from the dead.

After the Rosary, people shared stories. My sister Amy was the first to get up to speak. She reminisced about how Kevin was in Missouri with her at a football game where her husband worked as the athletic director. Racial tensions had been running high in the area. Kevin got off the elevator and gestured to a large Black man with a slight nod of his head which seemed to say, "Come on. Show me what you got." My sister freaked out. *How do I explain this to my husband?* she thought. But instead of trouble, the Black man replied with a friendly "Alright," then he and Kevin ran up to each other, bumped chests, and hugged. A show of team support. Everyone around them smiled as Kevin broke all the tension in the room so innocently. He was just excited for a game!

That was Kevin in a nutshell. A love for everyone and a love for the game.

One friend talked about how she loved going to the Best in the West Nugget Rib Cook Off with Kevin outside of Reno, Nevada. Every year, Kevin would hype friends and family to join him for the annual rib fest, and she laughed recalling how Kevin's face was always covered in BBQ sauce because he was enjoying it so much.

That, too, was Kevin in a nutshell. Loving life, wearing it all over his face.

His best friend Jordan stood up.

"In college in Sacramento, I was struggling to make friends, but then I met Kevin. I remember telling my mom about him. He's so funny, just hilarious. He was always bringing the party and the fun. One time, we went to a casino and as we walked in, Kevin challenged me: 'Let's count the number of mullets we see.' You know, the hairstyle where the hair is shorter in the front and longer in the back? Business in the front, and party in the back." They counted something like twenty-four.

And that was Kevin. Living life out loud.

I got up to speak. "I was so proud of Kevin because everyone knew how he felt about them. He told us all how much he loved us, and what we meant to him. He was always expressive emotionally." I recalled his cousin telling me she felt special to him because he would always call out to her, "Hey, buddy!"—making her feel like she was his special buddy.

Everyone felt like that. We were all his special buddy.

Later, we'd install a cement bench by his gravesite. On it, we'd inscribed, Love you, Buddy.

It was how we all felt about Kevin. Love. That night we laughed, we cried, we talked, we hugged.

Kevin would be missed.

And missed by more than just his friends and family. In the days leading up to his funeral, I contacted his psychiatrist, his therapist, and his neurologist to let them know Kevin would never be returning for another appointment. His doctor called me personally to express his sorrow. "The whole office cried when I told them he'd died. He was one of a kind."

His psychiatrist was also rattled. "I've never lost a patient before. I always looked forward to seeing him when I saw he was on my schedule." Then he couldn't keep talking; he had to get off the phone because he was too upset.

Kevin's therapist was also shocked. "Every once in a while, you get a client who you really enjoy. Kevin was one of those special ones. I can still see his bright eyes."

My heart was filling up from all the kind, loving words and stories about Kevin. His life mattered. He mattered to people. It was so important for me, as a bereaved mother to know others cared about Kevin, that he had so positively impacted other people's lives. It's how I want him remembered—for his love and generous heart, not for the tragic circumstances of his death.

The day before the funeral, my friend, a stylist, called me.

"What should I wear to the funeral?" I asked.

"Oh, Brenda," she replied. "It's not about fashion."

But that wasn't my point. I didn't know what to wear, not because I didn't know what was appropriate, but because I couldn't think at all. I just wanted someone else to pick out a dress and shoes and say, "Here you go."

Carmen understood. "What do I wear to my dad's funeral?" she'd asked.

I just didn't know.

The day of the funeral, I grabbed a black dress and some boots. Lori fixed my hair, and my other sister Jeanne did my makeup because they saw I wasn't capable. *How could I continue with normal, everyday, mundane tasks like clothes and hair and makeup when I was on my way to my son's funeral?*

The funeral procession began at the back of the church as John, Danny, Kara, Lorena, Carmen, Ozzie, Mikey, and I followed the casket to the front of the church, where we had the first two pews. I was barely breathing, shock and disbelief were the only things propelling me forward.

Our friends Mary and Patrick took care of the music. "We've played at masses and funerals for years," they reminded me. Their choices were beautiful. I remember one song in particular that they chose, the African American spiritual "Give Me Jesus." The song touched me deeply, especially because Kevin had loved it.

The priest gave a sermon on not knowing the answers to the question *why*, about not understanding when a young person dies. The unfairness of his death at such a young age was evident even to the priest, and his message was beautiful and comforting.

As we received communion, we walked right next to the casket, which the pallbearers had covered with the white cloth known as the pall. It looked so pure, yet so final. Each of us touched the casket as we passed by, a gesture that indicated we knew his body was with us, but he was no longer here.

This can't be real, I kept thinking as I went through the motions of honoring his life. This can't be the end of the story.

When the mass ended, Kara gave the first eulogy. She talked about how Kevin had a nickname for everyone. He called her "Time," which had been reduced from a silly saying he had about her; Danny was "Mizane," for which there is no explanation; I was "MaTiny"; his grandmother, who passed away a few years earlier, was "MaBig"; my husband was "Johnny D"; Paul, his uncle and best friend, was "Junior," meaning he was like his dad, Kevin's grandfather.

Kara also reminded everyone how he never passed you without a fist bump. She talked about what a great father he was to Carmen, connecting with her, taking her out for special talks, and to Ozzie, whom he loved to hang out with. And how much Kevin adored his baby. Kara also shared how he called her "spirit girl" because of her love for the holidays. "But he was the real spirit person," she concluded, her voice full of love and sadness. "He was the one who brought excitement and enthusiasm to everything, everywhere he went."

She had never been more right.

Crying, Danny got up to share his eulogy. He talked about how Kevin always annoyed him but now he wished he was still here annoying him. Kevin liked to tease his little brother. He shared about their different interests and while they were many years apart in age, they could always find common ground on things like music. Then he had the whole funeral laughing: "I know Kevin is saying right now, 'Dan, how did this become about you?'"

It was the levity we needed to survive this day.

My heart swelled with pride at the love and tenderness Kara and Danny showed for their brother. They wanted to talk. They wanted to honor Kevin. They were open and vulnerable in front of others, and it was beautiful. These special people found their own way to honor Kevin, and I could almost feel him receiving the love. I could almost imagine him embracing them in thanks.

My emotions were scattered throughout the funeral. Deep love and pride would give way to deep loss and hurt that then morphed into an indescribable numbness overwhelming me in grief. As we walked out of the church, I remember grabbing John's hand. I needed an anchor because I was lost in this nightmare and could not be tethered to the earth. I needed to hold on for support and steadiness. The connection to his body felt like the only thing holding me together.

Later, people would tell me they were at the funeral, that they'd offered condolences, but I had no memory. I felt like I should have been embarrassed at my lack of recall, but I wasn't. It had been all I could do to make it through the day.

We went to the cemetery next, watching woefully as the pallbearers struggled to carry the bulky casket across the grounds. Kevin had been a big guy, and the casket itself was heavy. They struggled with the literal—and metaphorical—weight of it all. As the mortuary staff lowered Kevin into the ground, Lorena asked if they could open the casket so she could put in flowers and a picture from their wedding. At first, the men hesitated, but how do you refuse a young widow and a dead man's baby? As they opened the casket, I didn't have the foresight to look away and my gaze settled on Kevin. His face was already changing color and beginning to decay.

It was another shock, another unreality.

After the burial, we headed back to the church for a reception where we had a buffet of Mexican food serving many of Kevin's favorites like pork carnitas, enchiladas, and chips and salsa. Kevin had befriended the owners of this new restaurant and they were happy to be a part of the reception. In the background, a photo montage cycled on a screen with Bob Marley and Mariah Carey songs on repeat.

The day after the funeral, we all headed up to a beautiful winery in the foothills of the Sierra Nevada Mountains. It was a perfect October day, the view was spectacular, the sun, just the right feeling of warmth on your skin. We got some food and wine. Kevin would have loved it.

"Kevin brought us all together," Susan, my sister-in-law, said as she took another sip of wine.

She was right. It was a love fest. I wanted it to last forever.

My sweet baby boy at 6 months

Kevin and me showing special bond at age 6

Danny and Kevin on his 27th birthday

Kevin and Kara confirmation

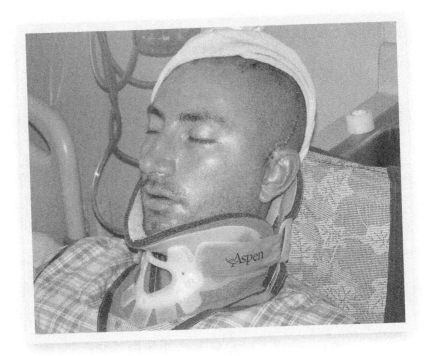

Kevin head injury

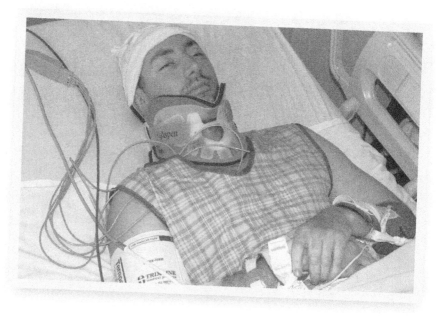

ICU

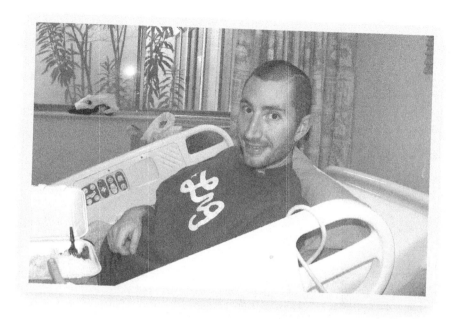

Acute rehab

Kevin on his wedding day

Mother/son dance

Kevin and Mikey

CHAPTER 23

Healing through Community

A few days after the funeral, I stopped by the church to have some masses said for Kevin, a Catholic tradition. The woman at the front desk told me how her only son had died of a virus less than a year before.

She's breathing, I thought as I tried to make sense of what she was saying. She was functioning, whereas I was barely able to get through the day.

I mumbled thanks and started toward the door but I couldn't leave without asking her an incredibly important question, "How have you survived?" I had to ask.

She took a moment to think of her answer. I could see compassion well up in her eyes. She shared that she had attended a bereaved parents conference the summer after her son had passed. She explained that she had traveled all the way across the country to attend, and talked about how helpful the workshops had been. If an organization like that helped this one woman, could it help me? I was desperate for something to get me through this grief. Immediately, I drove home to look up the organization. It turned out they had a local chapter, and I called that afternoon. An organizer, Chris, answered the phone.

Thank God someone picked up, I thought. I didn't think I would have had the energy to call back.

Chris invited me to have lunch with her. It was a gray, cloudy day, and matched the bleakness I felt inside. My body was present, but my heart was bleeding out, slowly, from excruciating, tormenting pain. Over barely touched salads, Chris sat with me for two hours and carried out the generous act of sharing her grief journey. Her son had died seven years earlier, and somehow, by God's grace, she had found the strength to carry on, largely because of the bereaved moms group of the local Bereaved Parents of the USA chapter she had joined. As I took in Chris's story, I was overwhelmed at the care, support, and attention she offered me. But what was most astounding was that she laughed. SHE SMILED. And right there, at that table, I felt the smallest seed of hope take root in my broken heart. Maybe, someday, I, too, would feel something other than absolutely shattered. She promised I would, but that it would take time. "The grief will always be with you, but the pain will diminish." Her eyes assured me I could trust her.

I was grateful to meet with a fellow bereaved mother. None of my friends had lost a child, none of my family. Until now, I had been alone in the world; an outsider, which, I've learned, only intensifies the feelings of loss. A deep loneliness weaves its way through your heartache. Loss of connection with my son turned into a loss of connection with others because nobody could understand this pain—except another mother who had lost a child.

Chris invited me to the next group in a few weeks. As the day approached, I started having second thoughts. I wasn't sure I wanted to be in a group right now. I didn't have the energy. Chris called to remind me about the meeting, and it was the same care and concern that she showed me at lunch that convinced me to go. I drove up to the house where the meeting was being held, already overwhelmed. I didn't want to be here. I didn't want to belong to a group of bereaved mothers. It would be too hard to talk about Kevin. It would make it all the more real. I could turn around. I could walk away. I would never have to speak to Chris again. Still, I made myself walk up to the house, and shuddered when I saw the Bereaved Moms sign. As I got closer to the door, I could hear them inside. I hesitated. My feet felt like I was carrying cement blocks and I just stared at the doorknob. I didn't want to go in. I didn't want to belong to a club no one wants to join. If I walked through that door, there was truly no escape. I would be forever labeled a "bereaved mother" and this nightmare was all going to be true. If I walked through that door, it meant Kevin was never going to walk back through the door of my house. I mean, I knew he was dead. I'd found him. But accepting the reality was another story. *I'll go this one time*, I rationalized to myself, *and I never have to come back*. I turned the doorknob. I walked inside. And did my best to keep breathing.

I was greeted by a few women who I'm sure could see I was dazed. The group's energy felt warm, and yet I was confused. There was laughter. *How could they be laughing at a time like this, with a group like this?* This obviously wasn't going to be for me.

There must have been about twenty women at the meeting that night, all in various stages of grief. Some were as newly bereaved as me, others had seven or more years of loss under their belt. I felt so out of place, which was an unfamiliar feeling. As a therapist, running groups had been one of my favorite things to do, but here, it felt different. We gathered in a circle to introduce ourselves, say our child's name, how long it had been since they died and, if we were comfortable, say how they died. The laughter ended. Each mother briefly shared their story. I could feel the anxiety rising in my throat. *I can't say it.* It felt like the dam was breaking open. My throat hurt. The words were stuck. My turn came, and I took a deep breath, voice quavering, and then just blurted it out to get it over with. "My name is Brenda. My son Kevin died a few weeks ago, on October 21. I'm not sure what he died of yet. We are waiting for the autopsy report."

I heaved a sob into the air. I said it. I spoke it. To a room full of strangers. I could have lied, pretended, made it all sound OK, but instead, I spoke the truth. Tears streamed down my cheeks, and by the end of the circle I knew I'd found my community. Everyone shared openly. Everyone had been shattered, cracked open, fragmented. We were all raw and vulnerable. We got each other—they got me, like no one had up until that point. They understood my pain, the numbness, the anger, the unfairness of it all, the profound, gut-wrenching loneliness. It was the deepest and most real connection I had ever experienced in my life. Of course Kevin would have brought me to this place. There was an instant intimacy, like we almost understood each other on a cellular level. Over time, I would find more solace in being together and sharing our stories, and most importantly, I would find a safe space to grieve. There was no "fixing" our grief, just a place where we could come and know we would be heard and understood. As the rest of the world moved on, I found the place where I could stand still.

CHAPTER 24

The Year of Firsts

The year following the death of a loved one is often referred to as a "year of firsts." Kevin's first birthday to be celebrated, as if in some sort of cruel twist of fate, was November 2, just barely two weeks after he died. We had only thirteen days to figure out how to live without him, and now, we had to celebrate his birth? Without him? Like being jolted with electricity, the waves of shock kept coming over me, leaving me reeling. We wrote notes of love on balloons and released them up to heaven. All we could do was hope he could hear us.

Then came our first Thanksgiving, about a month after he died. I didn't feel thankful for anything. Instead I was hollow inside, gutted. *Funny*, I thought, *like a Thanksgiving turkey, my inner parts felt like they had been removed.* And like the turkey, I, too, had once been a living, breathing animal of sorts. Now I was butchered and empty. We all went through the motions to keep the holiday tradition alive for the kids. We felt it was necessary to provide structure since our world and especially theirs had been turned upside down. But, it felt flat and forced.

Before we could process the pain of a holiday without Kevin, Christmas was upon us. Another first to endure. I couldn't bear hearing holiday songs or going to the mall to buy Christmas gifts. It was more than just grating, it was excruciating, like the sounds of countless jingle bells, a song I used to sing with Kevin when he was little. All those Christmas carols are about happy times, gathering together, being with family. It tore me apart. The grandkids came over with their parents as was our usual tradition. We opened gifts and ate a holiday meal. It was a repeat of the holiday just a month before—empty, void, feelingless.

That first Christmas night without Kevin was, in all honesty, the darkest night of my life. I felt so alone as my friends, with intact families, celebrated with their loved ones. I couldn't stop picturing their happy Christmases playing out in my mind. Their day was filled with hope and love and everything I wanted. All I wanted was Kevin back and that was impossible. As soon as everyone left, I collapsed on my bed from the exhaustion of it all. I was bone weary, but my body felt as if it was thrashing inside, and in my mind I was screaming, *No! No! No!* I was too broken to even weep and everything just grew darker. I didn't know how I would survive this unbearable, inescapable grief. I was being consumed by it.

And as I laid, motionless on my bed, considering how I was going to live with this pain, I heard my phone ding. A text message had come through.

"I'm thinking of you."

One text from a friend who had remembered me—and more specifically, acknowledged my pain—pierced through my darkness. It was a pinhole, and there wasn't much light. But it was something. Before I could think of how to respond, in came another.

"I'm thinking of you."

Such simple yet profoundly meaningful words from two dear friends. They took time away from their holiday with family to let me know they were with me in spirit. They let me know they understood I was in darkness. *Let there be light.* Those words came to me as I rolled over and sobbed into my pillow. It was the beginning of learning how to live without him.

CHAPTER 25

The Coroner's Report

Weeks passed and we still had not received any information from the coroner, though the office said it could take up to nine months because they were behind on reports. Still, I called them in February, frustrated and anxious for the results. The toxicology was in, but the coroner's report had not been completed. I begged for answers. I explained to them the pain of not knowing his cause of death. A few days later, the coroner kindly called me to explain that Kevin had died of a mixture of fentanyl and amphetamine, which had proven lethal because of his enlarged heart.

Fentanyl. I tried to catch my breath.

"He was afraid of fentanyl," I said in response to the coroner as if that changed anything. "He never would have used fentanyl," I explained.

Fentanyl kept going around in my brain on a loop. I couldn't unhear it, but I also couldn't believe what I was being told. I had begged him never to take any drugs from friends or acquaintances. We both knew the risks. Young people were dying every day from taking fentanyl thinking they were taking something else.

Kevin, you are a statistic now.

I was in shock.

"The amount of fentanyl in his system was not enough to kill him. It was a minimal amount. He did not have toxic levels of any drugs in his system. The small amount of fentanyl interacted with another medication. Do you know if he took something like Sudafed for a cold?"

"No, but he did have a cold. He may have taken some cold medicine. I just can't believe I'm hearing he took fentanyl."

"He didn't take it to get high. He didn't have enough in his system to get high. He took it for pain."

He took it for pain.

After all those months, after all his efforts to stay clean for Lorena, to reclaim his family . . .

"I just don't know why he would take something that wasn't prescribed," I tried to make sense of the news. "He knew the dangers."

"People with chronic pain do desperate things."

I wanted to throw up. I wanted to scream and cry. *How did she know he suffered so much from pain?* I had never spoken to her before. She went on to explain that she could see from the autopsy that he had been living with immense chronic pain because a significant amount of his brain tissue had turned brown and discolored—all of that a result of his accident. I wondered how he functioned as well as he had with such significant brain damage. I had no idea how bad it was.

It took a few more weeks to get the written report. The final case summary read as follows: "Cause of death: Toxic effects of fentanyl and amphetamine. Other Significant Conditions: Dilated cardiomyopathy. Based on the circumstances and cause of death, the manner will be listed as: Accident."

In another part of the report it states: "Describe how injury occurred: The descendent took drugs."

There it was in black and white. And those words haunted me. Kevin had been in so much pain. I could see the dark circles under his eyes. He was exhausted and spent. He had been through so much. Yet none of that context was in the report. The descendent took drugs. That was all.

Right after he died, I had done my own investigation. I knew he had been to the gym twice that last day, so I had called both gyms where he had memberships to ask for any information. I explained he died suddenly after working out twice the previous day. One of the gyms had no record of him being there on Saturday. The other gym acknowledged he had been there. The receptionist then said the strangest thing to me which, not understanding at the time, I'd stored away in the back of my mind.

"We can say he came into the gym, but we cannot say what happens in the parking lot."

Only after the coroner's report came in, could I see that the receptionist had been trying to tell me something indirectly. I later learned some bodybuilders have a reputation for taking pain medication, and I suspected someone in the gym had given Kevin something.

Lorena had been able to give us access to his iPad with his password, which helped us locate phone numbers of his friends. We got a record of his calls made on the Saturday before he died. All the calls were identifiable except one number. He'd called it several times around the time he said he was going to work out. Someone either met him at the gym or in the parking lot.

Kevin had bought one pill. One. One pill that, I would later learn, cost ten dollars. And this was why, when I'd found his body, he had only two dollars in his backpack.

With the phone number and my ability to track the number online, I could see the person lived in Sacramento. I wanted to call and scream, *You killed my son! You took the life of a father, a son, a brother. You have no right to sell drugs!* That guy got to live his life without knowing the destruction he left behind.

And it had all been so preventable.

It never had to end this way.

I did go to the police with the number and the information I had gathered. They looked up the number, which turned out to be known to them. They wanted to break into Kevin's phone to see if they could get exact text messages implicating this person. Unfortunately, Kevin's phone had been wet when we found it; we suspect Kevin had accidentally dropped it into the toilet as he was succumbing to the drugs. With the phone destroyed, the police couldn't do anything. The detective I talked to was so kind as he tried to explain, "The guy who sold your son the pill probably didn't know it had fentanyl." He believed the pill had probably been marked Norco, which made sense to me, since Kevin had often been prescribed Norco. He wouldn't have hesitated to take it, and it validated to me that Kevin would never have knowingly taken fentanyl. Kevin must have trusted the guy, especially since he was desperate for pain relief.

Still, it's too common of a story.

"The most you could hope for," the detective continued, "is a slap on the wrist, taking the guy off the street for a short time. It would have been nice to get more information about the bigger dealer, the one who supplied Kevin's friend."

That was it.

There was nothing else to do.

No one would be held responsible.

CHAPTER 26
The School of Grief

Grief and grieving continued to dominate my life; everyday tasks continued to prove difficult. In the mornings, I would make a list of things to do, a long-established habit of mine. Usually, I love creating a list of things I want to accomplish—I'd go off to complete the task and feel such a sense of satisfaction from the act of checking off the completed tasks as I went about my day that it was almost addictive. After losing Kevin, I would find my pen, lifeless in my hand, until I could manage to write only, *brush teeth* and *take shower*. Many days I could not even accomplish those tasks.

I did not succumb entirely to the grief. I knew I needed to figure out how I was going to get up so I could take care of the family that remained. I watched Mikey one day a week while Lorena returned to work, and slowly, I emerged, and engaged in life again. It would take more than a year before I felt like I was beginning to be present again, but it was possible.

My profession was the impetus to my resilience. Not everyone follows that path as they try to survive their grief, but for me, the more I could learn, the more I could help myself by seeing there was hope on the other side of this crushing heartache. As a clinical social worker, I was required to complete continuing education units every two years to keep my license. Taking courses in my field has always been one of my most favorite things about my job as a lifelong learner of human behavior. Now, it became a passion.

I received a brochure in the mail one day for a continuing education course in Sacramento. The course was "On Death and Dying," presented by a renowned grief expert, David Kessler. He had coauthored books with Elisabeth Kübler-Ross, a pioneer in the field of death and dying, in addition to writing his own books on loss. Given how much my bereavement group helped me, I was curious about what David Kessler would say on the subject, especially having read that his own son had died the year before. I wondered if I would feel connected through our pain when I sat in his audience. I wanted him to give me answers to how I could deal with the pain of my loss.

The seminar was held in a huge hotel ballroom. David was a popular speaker with a gentle and inviting style which drew a lot of clinicians interested in helping clients in grief. He covered all kinds of topics including different types of grief, feelings that come up in grief, spirituality, and even visits from our loved ones. He never mentioned his son, though I searched him for clues. He looked thinner than his picture and his cheeks appeared sunken in, but it did not seem to impact his presentation. He spoke with a certainty I didn't think possible for a grieving father—I must have gotten that information wrong; maybe it was another David Kessler.

Then, as the day-long seminar came to a close, David shared that his younger son had died. He had been only twenty-one, and it was sudden and unexpected. His son had been in recovery but had relapsed. David explained he felt his life was shattered. He'd had to attend grief groups himself because even a grief expert felt he could not deal with the loss of his son without support.

It was like David had been reading my own mind.

And as he continued to share about the experience of losing his son, I realized we were both doing the same things in order to keep surviving the tidal wave of grief. We were searching for meaning. As a way of surviving the loss of his son, David threw himself into writing a book. In it, he described *finding meaning* as the sixth stage of grief using Kübler-Ross's five stages of denial, anger, bargaining, depression, and acceptance as the base. As he continued to struggle after the loss of his son, he did not feel that his grief experience could conclude with acceptance. He found that his own survival was dependent on finding meaning after the loss of his child.

As I sat there in the audience, surrounded by social workers, parents, grief counselors, and psychologists, tears rolled down my face as I soaked up the powerful validation in his message. It felt like a proverbial fork in the road for me. My grief journey was asking me to make a choice: I could start down a path that would allow me to follow my curiosity and create meaning as a way of healing, or I could continue down the path of loss and allow the darkness to swallow me alive. His story made me want to continue living.

Because more than anything, I learned that day in his seminar something I desperately needed to believe:

We are not alone

When I came back from hearing David speak, I started reading everything I could get my hands on about grief. I became a student of grief.

One of the first and most powerful books I read was *Bearing the Unbearable: Love, Loss, and The Heartbreaking Path of Grief* by Joanne Cacciatore, PhD. I felt it was pure luck when I found her through a random search on Amazon for books on grief. Joanne's book put words to my feelings by acknowledging that, as bereaved mothers, our lives become unbearable. She writes, "When a person beloved by us dies, our lives can become unbearable. And yet we are asked—by life, by death—to bear it, to suffer the insufferable, to endure the unendurable."

Those words were enough for me, while they belonged to someone else, I felt a kindred connection, and that she had spoken for us all. She encouraged fully inhabiting the grief, allowing the feelings of grief to be present and move around inside me, rather than shutting them off and stuffing them down. So many well-meaning friends and family wanted me to move on, get over the pain, and rejoin life. They didn't want me to hurt because they also didn't want to be too close to such a horrific loss. They didn't want to get too close to the flame and see how real the pain is when you lose a child. In my most haggard and bottomed out moments, I could see I frightened them with my grief. As if it were contagious. *Bearing the Unbearable* named my grief for me at the time. And explained to me what I was doing: just bearing it.

The next book I read, *A Grace Disguised: How the Soul Grows through Loss* by Jerry Sittser, validated my questions about my faith and spirituality. The author's story about the loss of his wife, mother, and daughter in a tragic car accident recounts his loss of faith and questioning of God. Since I, too, had begun to wonder if God existed, his powerful words about his grief and the struggles he experienced also spoke directly to my own pain.

Later, I would read *It's OK That You're Not OK: Meeting Grief and Loss in a Culture That Doesn't Understand* by Megan Devine. This book was seminal because it gave me permission to grieve as I needed, and not to feel rushed to get over the loss of my son based on what convention, society, or other people in my life thought it should be. Devine wrote the words that I needed articulated, and in doing that, she acknowledged my loss, and didn't try to fix it. She didn't try to fix me. There was no fixing this. My new reality, a world without Kevin, was never going to be "fixed." Megan writes: "Here's what I most want you to know: this really is as bad as you think. No matter what anyone else says, this sucks. What has happened cannot be made right. What is lost cannot be restored. There is no beauty here, inside this central fact. Acknowledgement is everything. You're in pain. It can't be made better."

As my curiosity continued, it led me to a weekend retreat led by David Kessler. The retreat was meant to support the publication of his new book *Finding Meaning: The Sixth Stage of Grief*, which was the book he'd been working on when I'd first heard him speak. I made my way there, and I still think it was one of the best decisions I made in prioritizing my healing. The beautiful weekend gave me hope that I could find a way to make meaning out of Kevin's life. It was a nuanced approach to the topic; one which appealed to my own emotions. While most people would assume finding meaning after the death of a loved one is silver-lining thinking, it is, in fact, the opposite. It's not about finding meaning from their death—that would be like recognizing the death itself was somehow good and valuable, none of which I could see in Kevin's sudden demise. Instead, he taught us how to find meaning from their lives. It's about finding value in who they were and how they lived—what they brought to the world before their death and bringing that meaning—and therefore them—fully into the present. He showed us that it wasn't about letting go of our bond and that there was no moving on, but searching for meaning was more about bringing their heart and soul and spirit—the value of their lives—with us going forward.

Then Covid hit. The country—the world—was locked down. The strain, stress, and pressure affected everyone in different ways, but for those who were grieving, for those, like me, who relied on face-to-face support groups—the shutdowns were a blow. Grieving people had nowhere to turn, so David Kessler started an online group which met twice a week for about half an hour. He invited all kinds of people who had experienced loss to speak. Kim Goldman, whose brother was murdered with Nicole Brown Simpson, spoke about her grief journey. Christopher Reeve's son, Will Reeve, spoke about losing his father and mother. Natalie Wood's daughter, Natasha Gregson Wagner, shared about the loss of her mother. Rabbi Steve Leder, author of *More Beautiful Than Before: How Suffering Transforms Us*, discussed the loss of his father and the reflections he had compiled in his book. Many famous and not-so-famous people joined together to support anyone who had suffered a loss and needed support during the pandemic. Those videos were a lifeline for me. I would block out everything in that time period, and I would then sit and listen, absorb and learn. It was an incredible year of learning, a life-changing gift.

One speaker, Robert Neimeyer, the head of the Portland Institute for Loss and Transition, caught my attention. He spoke so gently and possessed so much knowledge and understanding about grief; I was drawn to his ideas on reconstructing a life of meaning after the death of someone you loved. I learned that, as a clinical social worker, I could take classes from the Institute—I didn't have to ponder that possibility for very long. At first, I signed up for just one class, I didn't want to overwhelm myself. Then, I signed up for another and then another. The model developed by Robert Neimeyer is called *meaning reconstruction*, which he talks about in the article, *Meaning Reconstruction in Bereavement: Development of a Research Program*. Neimeyer believes "a central process in grieving is the attempt to reaffirm or reconstruct a world of meaning that has been challenged by loss." I was attracted to the idea of meaning making. My life had not just been challenged by loss but shattered, and I wanted to find a way to rebuild my life, integrate the experience of my loss, and explore who I was now in the aftermath. Rebuilding my life through meaning felt like the answer.

After many courses were completed, I realized I had found my focus, and a reason to continue living. I decided to pursue a certificate in Grief as Meaning Reconstruction, and over the year and a half of classes, studying cases, and participating in mentoring, I began to coalesce my own grief. Whatever I learned, I applied to myself.

Then, David Kessler started a Grief Educator certificate program, another year-long training session. He included education on loss of a child, a parent, a sibling, a spouse. David covered death by suicide and drug overdose as well as deaths from an illness or accident. The certification program gave me a strong base of knowledge about all types of losses. My own experience of grief was reflected back to me by all the meetings in the certificate program, especially on loss from substance use.

I recognize that my own grief journey is not necessarily something that can become a template for others to follow. Many people may not be interested or emotionally capable of reading and researching like me, nor would they want to pursue the education path I did. But for me, it wasn't about the certificates; it was about the learning process. Learning about grief helped me understand what was happening to my soul. And that understanding became essential for my survival because it gave me the tools I needed to dig myself out of my own grave. Once I was able to stand on my own two feet again, I could walk toward the light that this community offered me. I was able to leave the isolation of my grief behind as I gathered with others who were committed to understanding the human experience of grief.

I know now my learning was a desperate attempt to try to make peace with the loss that nobody in the world outside of grief wanted to talk about. My extended family and friends would rather I have "gotten over it," but I needed to talk about my loss. I craved shouting it from the rooftops. They didn't understand that I was straddling two worlds because they were lucky enough to exist in just one. I, on the other hand, had to grapple every minute of every day with the both/and.

Life and death.

Darkness and light.

Despair and hope.

I needed to be with other people who also straddled those worlds. I needed them to show me how I would be able to survive.

CHAPTER 27

The Wreckage

Often, the death of a loved one can feel like a bomb exploding in a family, leaving victims in fragments, pieces flung all over the place. Acute trauma was the initial experience.

Shock and numbness.

Disbelief and distress.

Kevin's death sent all of us on a downward spiral as if a nuclear weapon had been aimed right at all our hearts.

For me, the acute trauma manifested in difficulty sleeping. Since I was the one who found Kevin dead in his bed, I couldn't close my eyes to sleep without the image of my boy, gray and unmoving, coming up behind my eyelids, forcing them open. Much like the image of Kevin the first time I held him as a newborn, the image of him lying dead in his bed would be forever burned in my mind. During the day, I could distract myself from the visuals of his death but, at night, it was a different story. I would sit straight up in bed, my nightgown drenched in sweat, heart racing from the anxiety of reliving his death over and over in recurring nightmares. I could hardly utter complete sentences because of the exhaustion but still, I could not sleep. Most nights, I would stay up into the early hours of the morning until finally collapsing into sleep somewhere around four from sheer exhaustion. I'd sleep until eight or nine, and as I'd roll out of bed and check my To Do list reminding myself to brush my teeth or take my shower, I would have a renewed sense of appreciation for all the sleep issues Kevin experienced after his injury.

I didn't have an appetite. There was no desire for food, and if I did want to eat, I would catch myself right before experiencing pleasure at the taste or texture of what had once been a favorite meal, feeling guilty because Kevin couldn't be there to enjoy it with me. Instead of thinking of food, I would watch the clock, checking it every hour for the entire afternoon until it hit five o'clock so I could have my nightly cocktail. Crown and Coke. Just one. It helped to take the edge off. My grief would go from feeling like I was going to crawl out of my skin to a dull thud of painful heartbreak. I've never been a big drinker nor a daily drinker, but during the first month, I looked forward to numbing some of the pain with alcohol. One night, over said cocktail, I confided in a friend my concern.

"I can't eat a thing, but all I can think about all afternoon is getting to five o'clock so I can have my Crown and Coke." I felt so ashamed, given the history of alcoholism in my family. My heart let out its own sigh as she normalized the craving for me; she assured me it was okay for now, reassuring me this would pass. And she was right. After sharing my concern with her, I dropped the nightly drink and returned to being the occasional social drinker. I was relieved when the desire left me. Turning to alcohol never seemed like the best choice. In fact, I was sure it was pushing down feelings I needed to process. I watched with compassion as some of my fellow bereaved moms turned to alcohol for years. It was predictable, and yet, I was surprised as I watched their physical and mental health decline.

Weekly therapy began to help me deal with my loss. I needed someone to share all my thoughts and feelings with who wasn't a family member—each of them were going through their own nightmares of losing Kevin, and they had enough to deal with in managing their own feelings about the loss. During therapy, I uncovered the disturbing reality that one of my greatest fears was losing another child. My therapist normalized this fear by explaining that it was a common concern for a parent, especially after losing someone suddenly. My innocence of a world that would not take away my family had been stripped away. It had happened once, what was to keep it from happening again?

And my fear of losing another child was not unfounded. Danny had been living with us while finishing college when Kevin died. With my help and the support of his teachers, he finished that semester about six weeks after Kevin passed. Then, he completed his final semester, graduating that spring.

But Danny had been struggling with himself and the loss of his brother. Finishing college brought other feelings of loss and transition; of, *What now, what next?* I'm sure he felt the pressure to get a job, to be successful, to perform as an adult. Yet he was not ready to make all those decisions, and he hadn't really had any time to grieve the loss of Kevin. Instead of taking the time to deal with his loss, Danny put his whole focus on finishing school. Stuffing his feelings inside led Danny into a deep depression, and eventually alcohol—he was in free fall.

Danny had never really partied in high school but when he turned twenty-one, alcohol became a new and interesting experience for him. He, like most young adults, discovered alcohol provided a filter for reality, and he could fit in. Danny started drinking more, and not just when he was with friends. When I went into his room, I found numerous empty bottles lying around. John and I confronted Danny about his drinking, trying to help him understand that alcoholism ran in both sides of the family.

"It's in your DNA. You need to be careful," we would plead.

"Mom, I'm okay. I just need it to relax. I've got it under control."

I didn't think it was okay. I was observing a problem developing quickly—I was watching history repeat itself.

And yet again, I felt powerless.

When Kevin died, Danny's drinking escalated, and he began consuming bottles of wine alone in his room. My once vibrant and hilarious son evolved into a recluse and was depressed and angry.

"Please. Please, stop drinking. I can't handle losing another child."

I begged and pleaded. I cried and cajoled. As Dan's drinking continued with nightly binges behind closed doors, I lived in terror.

Dan had struggled with anxiety and depression for a while and started on a new medication to help relieve these symptoms. It is never a good idea to mix medication with excessive alcohol, and I was worried. John and I noticed Dan had been repeatedly sleeping all day, which obviously was a huge trigger for me. About to lose myself in panic, John and I waited until just past noon one day before we both started banging on Danny's door. I banged until the side of my fist hurt. No answer.

I jiggled the doorknob. I didn't care about his privacy at that moment. My heartbeat was almost audible. The door was locked. We continued banging, taking turns shouting his name through the thick wood door, screaming at the top of our lungs. Still no answer.

"Dan! Dan! Wake up! Answer me!" My throat cracked from the pressure of realizing what I might find on the other side of the door.

After what felt like an eternity, we heard a "What?" shouting from Dan's sleepy voice. I sighed in relief, and then erupted in anger. *Didn't he realize what he was putting us through?*

"Open the door!" I demanded—I was seeing red now. "You are never allowed to lock this door ever again!" The emotion of the whole ordeal had gotten the best of my logic.

He was twenty-two; as if we could have stopped him. But we tried, again, to explain to him how terrified we were of losing him. Yet his downward spiral continued because his disease was progressing.

A few weeks later, I found myself on the outside of his bedroom door again. It was quiet, so I followed my gut and entered his room. He had been drinking excessively that evening, and I couldn't rouse him from sleep. I took immense relief in the fact that I could see his chest rising and falling, but I still picked up my phone and dialed the on-call nurse, who listened to my fears and explained he could be having a reaction to mixing his medication with alcohol.

I sat down on the edge of Danny's bed and closed my eyes—all I could see was Kevin lying lifeless.

I was finally able to wake him up, but the on-call nurse requested he be seen in the ER, and the doctor decided to keep him overnight. The next morning, I picked him up from the hospital and was met with his fury. He unleashed on me in the car for taking him to the hospital when he was just drunk, and, upon stopping at a coffee shop so he could get a cup of black coffee to help him sober up, his anger was apparent to a young woman who was going into work. She approached the car to check on me.

"You don't deserve that," she stated with concern, motioning to my son, standing in line waiting for his coffee.

Wow. A stranger in a parking lot could see the truth of what was going on. Her words of compassion struck me: I didn't deserve this.

In spite of all our conversations and efforts to intervene, Dan's binge drinking continued. My therapist was as concerned as I was that Danny was going to die from drinking. And all the while, I could barely function through my own grief.

I began searching for treatment programs that would address Danny's issues. I found one in Los Angeles, and one of the therapists talked me through ways we could start encouraging Danny to get treatment. I planned to confront Dan with his options; I just needed to get through the second anniversary of Kevin's death.

The day after the anniversary, without any prompting from me, Dan came to my bedroom. "Mom, I need help."

I nearly fell out of my bed. I didn't realize he was beginning to see he had a problem with alcohol.

He had found a treatment program on his own and called them. It was an outpatient facility, which I didn't think was the best option, but I was willing to support his choice. Still, I explained what I had come up with. "I've been talking to a program in LA where you would live for two months. Give them a call. I support whatever program you choose."

By the following day, Dan was on a flight to LA, where he has continued to grow and blossom in his recovery.

Such a weight off my shoulders. I knew we would always have struggles in our family, but in the midst of trying to cope with my own grief, I was relieved Dan was getting the help he needed.

Danny wasn't the only one who struggled. All of us were broken and shattered.

It took years to begin to glue ourselves back together piece by piece.

CHAPTER 28

Before and After

Before Kevin was born, I was a young, adult woman figuring out my way in the world. After Kevin's birth, I entered the new realm of motherly love; indescribable, unconditional—it's a love which gave me my life's meaning and purpose. The after was life altering, but I've learned that altered life can be a slice of heaven on earth.

Before Kevin's head injury, life was relatively normal. We had our bumps in the road, but life was generally good. After the head injury, Kevin changed, and I grieved for the Kevin I knew, but that was gone. Ambiguous loss. But, I could learn to live with the deficits. The after was painful, but also full of love and many good times. I still had Kevin so there was always that blessing. He was still here.

Time stopped when Kevin died.

The before and after were divided into that hard reality. Kevin lived. Then, Kevin died. A strong line of demarcation separating the before and after.

After is not just the empty place at the table or the text messages that no longer come. It's not just the I love you's that will never be said again, or warm embraces that will never be felt. A whole person is gone from your life. And the hole is so big, it splits you in two; you become a before and an after as well.

In the beginning, the after feels as if the grief is like cancer, it grows and morphs, until it takes over your mind. It's the only thing you can see, it's the only thing you can think about. Every morning I went through the same progression: the goneness. That's how I describe life in the after. Everywhere you go, there are constant reminders your loved one is gone. In time, the grief becomes your companion, moving into the emptiness your lost one has left, keeping you company. At first you want it to go away—like a dark shadow, it follows you into every room of your house, into every moment of your life, until you surrender. You stop fighting it and you allow it to stay. Acceptance, stage five, of grief. You recognize the pain will always be with you.

Billy Bob Thornton best described long-term grief in an interview he gave about living with the loss of his brother by explaining, "There's a melancholy in me that never goes away. I'm 50 percent happy and 50 percent sad at any given moment." I understand that on a level that I cannot explain. Before, I was whole in some way; 100 percent happy when I was happy, 100 percent sad when I was sad. Now, I'm never 100 percent of anything. And the funny thing is, you don't know you are whole until half of you goes missing. I'll never be the same again.

CHAPTER 29

Guilt and Grieving in the Brain

I couldn't save him. And you can see, I tried. But no one could save him.

For years afterward, guilty thoughts haunted me:

If only I asked more questions.

If only I had checked on Kevin or taken more time to talk to him that night.

What if I had begged him or pleaded more or insisted on inpatient treatment?

What if I had been a better, more attentive mother?

What if I just made him my number one priority?

Was it that his biological father left before he was born?

Should I have done something different as a single mother?

I would relive the what-ifs and if onlys of all the decisions I had made from the day I found out I was pregnant to the day he died. I'd relive Kevin's childhood, examining it in excruciating detail. I'd search our entire lives together, sure I'd find the moment when I could have chosen differently. Through my studies, I discovered parents who lose a

205

child almost always feel guilt for not being able to save them. I've heard parents of children who died of cancer claim it was their fault, because they failed to get them to the doctor soon enough. Parents of children who die by suicide or drugs believe they could have somehow prevented it if they had just caught more of the signs. When a parent has a child die, it hardly matters the age, they will always look back with regret, believing they will uncover the moment they did something wrong. They do this because it gives them a sense of control; they want to fix it so they can rewrite the ending. Desperate to change the outcome, hindsight is a real tease, because following that path will only lead to abject hopelessness. Like a hamster on a wheel, the coulda-woulda-shoulda loop, is a never-ending cycle of rumination that will drive you mad.

Parents aren't supposed to outlive their children; in a world that runs correctly, children don't die before their parents. Our whole belief about how things should be, has been turned upside down.

The randomness of Kevin's death shook me to my core. It may not seem random to others, given his history and medical condition, but for me it was the biggest shock of my life. We had spent his last day talking and laughing together. We enjoyed a few meals. Kevin and I had a meaningful exchange before he went to bed. Then, he was just… gone. I now had proof that I was powerless and helpless in this world and that I had no real sense of control.

In my grief studies, I have learned about counterfactual thinking, or, thoughts that run counter to the facts of what actually happened. The facts are simple. Kevin had a head injury. He suffered from chronic pain. He took a pill to relieve that pain, and he died. Those are facts. Grief causes us to use the what-ifs and if onlys as a way to conjure up an alternative outcome, and because we are in "control" we can create a positive one at that. An example of a counterfactual thought process could look like: Kevin doesn't die because I confront him, so he doesn't take the pill. The reality is, maybe I could have saved him that night, but his chronic pain and his brain damage may have led him to resort to the same pain management on another night. The truth is I couldn't control his choices. I couldn't fix the brain injury. I couldn't fix his relationship with his wife. I couldn't fix his addiction to pain medication. I couldn't be the functioning part of his brain for him. The fact is, he died.

Mary-Frances O'Connor, PhD, gives two reasons in her book, *The Grieving Brain: The Surprising Science of How We Learn from Love and Loss*, for why our brains engage in counterfactual thinking. First, our brains want to prevent other deaths in the future. Our instincts kick in and want to protect us and other people from more loss. If we believe it is our fault, not only could we have fixed it, but we could also prevent future losses, and therefore, future pain.

The second reason our brains engage in counterfactual thinking is to avoid the gut-wrenching truth that our loved one is gone. It takes the brain a long time to accept that reality. If we stay stuck in the what-ifs and if onlys, it distracts us from doing the work required to accept that our loved one is never coming back.

The Grieving Brain helped me understand how my brain was doing counterfactual thinking to keep me safe. It wanted to protect me from the horrible reality I was living without Kevin. No amount of coulda, shoulda, woulda was going to bring him back. I realized I could stop blaming myself for all my real or imagined failures as a mother. If I had done something different, if he had done something different, if his friend hadn't sold him the pill, if there had been a better solution for his chronic pain—it didn't matter now. The fact is Kevin died. The fact is he is gone. The fact is, it hurts so much.

The book helped me see that guilt and regret come from an attempt to fix what happened, so that the survivor can regain control, so we don't have to face the pain. If we can figure out why, then no one else around us will die. Once I understood what my brain was doing, I was able to get past it. It wasn't me, specifically. I wasn't weak or hopeless or a terrible person because I was consumed with guilt; it was simply a survival mechanism; it was my brain trying to protect me, trying to keep me alive.

CHAPTER 30

Losing My Religion

One of the secondary losses of grief for me, was a loss of my faith, something I relied on for comfort and sustenance for most of my life. Raised in the Catholic faith tradition, my spiritual practice was a central part of my life. I wasn't always a church going Catholic, though. During college, I explored whether my faith was fitting for me and rarely attended mass. Having children changed all of that and I returned to the faith of my youth.

After Kevin died, I entered a dark, empty hole of loneliness. I couldn't feel God's presence. All I could feel was my anger at him for taking Kevin away. How could a God who loves me do this to me?

I quit going to church. As I laid awake in bed at all hours of the night, I doubted, in fact, that there was a God. I drifted away from my faith-based friends. I couldn't bear to hear them talk about God's will for Kevin. *How could this pain I was experiencing be the will of God?*

Ironically, in the early days after Kevin died, I actually felt close to my faith. It almost seemed I was floating in between the thin veil that separated heaven and earth. When I went to mass, the priest's words penetrated my heart, opening me up to experience the powerful presence of God in my life. The love that surrounded us during Kevin's funeral was spirit-filled and the love fest that followed filled me with deep faith.

Then, one day it stopped. I just woke up, and the peace I had been feeding from had been swallowed up and there was no more left. Pain and grief took over in its absence and it was unbearable. I prayed for relief and begged for mercy. There was only silence on the other end of my prayers. I had prayed for Kevin after his accident, during his recovery from his TBI, in the midst of his addiction. I pleaded with God for help.

I wanted to throw up when people would squeeze my hand and patronizingly offer, "God needed another angel."

No. He didn't.

"He's in a better place," they would say.

Really? A better place than with his family who loved him? Is there a better place than the one where Kevin could watch his son grow and thrive?

"Everything happens for a reason."

Fuck off! I'd think as I stared coldly into the offender's eyes. There is no good reason for Kevin to be gone. And you know it.

People want to give you a nice little platitude, wrap up your pain with a bow, and make it palatable. For them. *Spiritual bypassing*, they call it. Let's just bypass all these painful feelings and slap on a nice God phrase. Spiritual bypassing minimizes the depth of the griever's feelings. It takes all the complex emotions of grief and offers a simple, spiritual explanation meant to put a safe distance between the reality of what has happened, and the reality that this could happen to them one day too. "Here, let me tell you God's plan for you and Kevin. It will help you." But what they really mean is, it will help *them*. These comments, intended to help me find the silver lining in my horrific loss, only pushed me further away from God.

I continued to join my friends for a rosary group once a month, for the sake of routine, but I couldn't pray. There was nothing left for me to say. But my friend's prayers somehow sustained me. Their belief held my unbelief, until it could be reexamined.

God was silent. And the silence was deafening.

Even in that deafening silence, I missed the security that came from a belief in a power greater than myself. I missed that power I could surrender to when I was in my greatest need. But I just couldn't trust in the kind of God that allowed this much pain in my heart.

In my ongoing search for answers, I ended up taking a free class from Yale called The Science of Well-Being. One of the assignments we completed involved keeping a gratitude journal that was meant to help rewire the brain. I was expected to write five things every day for which I was grateful. I didn't think it would be that hard, but a couple of weeks into the assignment, I found myself struggling to come up with five things I was grateful for. I thought about it for five minutes. What am I grateful for today? It's so hard to be grateful in grief. I decided I needed to get out of the house, so I went out to my backyard.

For the first time all summer, I noticed this beautiful, fuchsia-colored flower growing in my favorite blue pot in my backyard. My body had been in a permanent state of collapse; I was physically hunched over, buckling from the weight of the grief I was carrying. But when I stood up and moved around, this fuschia flower came into my line of vision, and I couldn't help but notice how vibrant it was. I literally felt my body lift. My head tilted back as if it was in control of itself and I noticed how green the trees were.

There's still beauty here, I thought.

It was a revelation. A turning point. The grief had stolen the color from my life, and everything I had been looking at had taken on the dark gray hue of death. In this moment, searching for gratitude as if my life depended on it, the gray dissipated, and I started seeing the world in color again.

There's something greater than me here.

Even now reflecting on that moment of change still brings me to tears. No one ever told me grief would turn my colorful life into a sad and lifeless gray. No one ever told me I would find color again. And that when I did, I'd hold onto that color for my own survival, determined to never lose it again. It was a spiritual awakening.

There's something greater than me.

Though I haven't regained the faith of my youth, in the same way that I haven't healed from Kevin's death, I've come to a place of openness about spirituality and other religions. I'm not locked into one thing anymore—there is no right religion and there is no wrong way to experience spirituality. I don't know what happens after we die, but I do know I'm just open to something greater than me. And I know that this place I'm in right now feels much better than the hopeless space I was trying to exist in before.

My spirituality is so much deeper and richer than it ever was, but I still struggle with trusting God fully, and that is okay with me now. Spirituality has taken on a new meaning for me. I have found a new spirituality based on our common powerlessness and brokenness.

Our common humanity.

CHAPTER 31
Resilience

When I completed the collage that brought me to my breakthrough, it was another major turning point in my grief journey. I was surprised because I saw my own resilience on paper, in black and white (and color). There it was—I got up. Even now, it makes me cry. I never thought I was going to be able to get up from that. When you lose a child, you think that you're never going to be happy. In fact, for a long time, you don't want to even let go of the pain of their loss. Letting go of the pain, you think, means you are letting them go too.

But as my life moved from black and white back into color, and as I began to rediscover a new, revised version of my spirituality, I came to a curiously different perspective. On the collage, I included a broken heart—it was how I felt. I had been feeling trapped in the impossible reality. Kevin's gone, Kevin's gone, Kevin's gone. But broken or not, my heart was still full of love for him. That never dissipated. The love didn't disappear just because my heart had been smashed into fragments. I discovered my love for Kevin was still fully alive in my heart, and in fact, my love for him had grown more. Kevin's spirit will always live in me.

It took me a while until I could name my resilience for what it was, but once I had, I wanted to get to know it better. The conventionally accepted definition of resilience—that we bounce back from adversity—didn't sit right with me. In my experience, that was not available in grief. Resilience within the grief experience felt different.

I dove back into my research and pondered those questions. Over time, I came to see resilience in grief through the lens of the dual process model of bereavement developed by Stroebe and Schut in 1999. On one side there is the loss orientation, where you feel the pain, where missing your child is a visceral experience. It's filled with sadness, despair, and desperation. Even years later, I could walk into a grocery store, hear Kevin's favorite song on the overhead speakers, and become overwhelmed by my loss. But, on the other side is restoration; this is the space in which you can manage your pain, a place where you can live in the present moment, and even experience a moment of joy, happiness, or simple pride in your efforts to show up for the other people in your life. This became relevant to me when I made a meal for my family— the first one I'd attempted to make—a few weeks after Kevin died. I made spaghetti. It was simple: a bagged salad, a jar of sauce with ground beef and noodles, but I made it. I remember standing in the kitchen thinking, *Wow, I made dinner.* It was huge. Though I couldn't recognize it at that very moment, later, I came to see it as a little restoration. I didn't stay in that mode, though, and that was my revelation.

Resilience in grief is about the oscillation between loss and restoration. It's a back and forth motion. For a long time, it feels like you're stuck in the loss; but, with my simple meal, I was able to experience a moment of restoration. As time passed, as I learned more about grief and sought out support from other bereaved parents, those moments in the restoration mode lasted longer, and when I did shift back into loss, the amount of time to swing again into restoration had lessened. That's what happens. We keep moving back and forth like that. Sometimes I'll be back in the sadness so deeply I can't even think straight, and then I'll shift back into restoration. Years later, I can stay longer in the restoration mode, but I believe I'll be oscillating for the rest of my life. It's a process, different for each of us. Some may linger longer in loss; others may find themselves in restoration sooner, but the idea that our lives can be both is what's relieving. We don't have to fear giving up our loved one by feeling a moment of joy. The loss will return. It's not going anywhere. We allow and accept that the pain will always be there, in some way, but we're also not locked in it. We can move on with our lives. We can have restoration too.

We are both.

Not either/or.

But and.

Loss and restoration.

This duality addresses the preconceived notion that you start out with grief, then go on a journey, and finally arrive at a destination where you're all healed, and now there's a nice little bow on it, ending your grief. Anyone who has experienced loss knows it doesn't work like that. We will never stop grieving our children. Some of the people I've met in bereavement groups have been participating for twenty or more years. According to the conventions of society, they should have already moved on, but everybody needs a place where they can talk openly and without judgment about the loss of their children. We honor all the kids, no matter how long ago they lived, and that's important to the parents. At the conferences I've attended, everyone wears a picture of their child, so you start to get to know the parents by the picture of their kid: *Tell me about your son. Your daughter. How old were they when they died? Tell me what happened. Tell me about them.* They're conversation starters in a safe environment, where we don't have to pretend we're always alright, that there's a timeline or a schedule we're all supposed to follow. It's a beautiful environment where our kids are important and valued and we can talk about them. We can say their name and by doing that, we remember them, and remembering them keeps our kids alive.

What's often difficult for the newly bereaved is the acceptance of ambiguity. We have to learn to live with it. The both-and philosophy. We're gutted from our pain, empty, and we can recall memories that fill our hearts with love. We've been through the darkest night, and we rebuild our lives with meaning and come into a new day. We want to both celebrate a wedding and feel the sadness that our child isn't there to witness it. It's never one or the other. I think that we all live in ambiguity, but I think in grief, it's even more essential that you learn how to find acceptance in that ambiguity. Life isn't cut and dried, and surviving the death of a loved one isn't either. There may be other people's experiences from which to draw for inspiration or guidance, but there are no rules. Once you can appreciate the inherent overlap of emotions, once you can recognize the duality of both your loss and your restoration, that's when you'll find your own resilience.

My newfound insight into resilience also led to the strength and determination to address other long-standing issues connected to Kevin's death. I continued to be plagued by recurrent nightmares of finding Kevin dead. Finally, I had the inner balance to address these issues and sought out a sleep specialist, who taught me to retrain my brain like training a puppy. Our brains, through neuroplasticity, have amazing abilities to find new pathways to help us heal. My brain just needed some help. No caffeine after a certain time; no computers after a certain time. They were simple things that we all know we should do, but now I had someone to whom I was accountable, and it helped.

These sleep exercises, plus my effort to walk more, and my new focus on practicing gratitude, are all resilient practices. I hadn't appreciated that before. Just the simple fact of saying something I'm grateful for every day is an act of resilience.

I couldn't have done it at the beginning. If someone had said write down what you're grateful for, I would have wanted to punch them right in the face. *How am I supposed to be grateful? Don't you get it, my son is dead!* You don't want to look at gratitude. You can't. You're not ready. The pain is too acute. As hard as it is, you have to get through that phase first. Since it's been years since Kevin's death, I find myself in a different phase now, one I truly didn't believe existed, but I am living proof.

When I explain my path to resilience, in groups or speaking engagements, I get a positive response from people who are grieving.

"I don't want to believe this grief is going to consume me forever," they'll say, hopeful when they hear the dual process model of loss and restoration.

"Neither state is good or bad," I'll remind them. "It's just grief, and you're going to move between the two. When you're in the loss, allow it. When you're in restoration, allow it. Enjoy it, even, because you will go back to loss. You're not letting go of your loved one if you experience happy moments."

It comforts me, and others, too, because it's like we've been given permission to feel this way, that our emotions, no matter what they are, are valid.

Resilience also leads to another fundamental emotion: hope. I don't think it's possible at the beginning, when you're in the acute phase of your grief. You don't even want hope. Your pain is your connection to your loved one and you're terrified to let go of that. It may sound weird to those who have never experienced such profound grief, but it's true. When I would have those moments of relief, I would push them away. It was in pain that I felt closest to Kevin, and I was loath to give it up. Eventually, I would learn that grief isn't always about the pain, it's about the relief of love too.

For me, in the beginning, hope came for me in the stories from other mothers who had suffered a similar loss—the mothers that the picture of Jill Biden came to represent for me years later. They were standing up. They were laughing. They were surviving, and perhaps, they were thriving. At the time, it seemed too much of an impossibility that I would ever get there. But I did.

It's why I choose to reach out. I'll do talks locally or invite people from my group over to do a collage. I'll speak at conferences, and prepare workshops when I'm invited, and I'll make myself available to those in need. I have a Grief Educator Certificate for a reason. I want to help. I'm in this world, whether I want to be or not, and I have the training, so if what I do can offer some comfort, then that's worth it.

But honestly, my work helps me as much as it helps them. I learn so much. I put together a workshop on spirituality because I needed a workshop on spirituality. I put together a workshop on the grieving brain because I needed to understand the grieving brain. I put together a workshop on resilience because I needed to learn more about resilience. I suspect I'll be learning for years; every day I have to navigate my life without my son, and every day a new challenge may arise. The anniversary of his death, for example, or the milestones my grandson will celebrate without his father. But I've come a long way. I may swing back into loss, but I'm much more confident that I'll also end up in restoration.

Because I have hope.

CHAPTER 32

Kintsugi bowl

My own journey reminds me of *kintsugi*, the Japanese art of putting broken pottery pieces back together with gold. While I am not the first to appreciate the metaphor in embracing our own flaws, imperfections, challenges, struggles, and obstacles, the imagery resonates with me. I had been searching to bring myself back into a place of wholeness, but I soon learned what I had been striving for was impossible. How could I ever be whole without Kevin? For a long time, I thought that meant I'd never cope with the pain, but now I see it's not about shutting out the trauma; it's acknowledging it. We are all broken, in our own ways, but it's the way we put ourselves back together that lets our true beauty shine. Our own patterns—the cracks now laced with gold—will vary, but there is strength in the new form.

I was shattered, there's no question. My bowl had fragmented, broken into a million little pieces. My life—my kintsugi bowl—had to be pieced together starting with the bigger fragments. But even after gluing those together, my kintsugi bowl has a hole in it. Part of my bowl turned to dust, and there is no way to make it whole again, not even with gold.

In the beginning of our loss, we always hope that in the end, we'll still be the same as we were before but in reality, we will actually be changed forever. We can't be made into the same whole; we can only be reconstructed into another version. And it's the acceptance of no longer being the same whole that puts us on that path toward healing. And just because we've been broken, doesn't mean we can't still be useful.

As time passed, as I learned more about the fluctuation between loss and restoration, I began to see how my service to others was helping heal me. Service in the form of leading groups and doing talks got me out of myself and into the wider world. Grief narrowed my life for a time, but finally, I began to expand as I found ways to contribute, by teaching others what I have learned. It gave me purpose. Connection and service helped to heal my heart by sharing my story and listening to others. It gave me a reason to live.

My story may not be your story; my trauma may be different than yours. I experienced a type of loss when Kevin was injured in the accident, and I had to learn ways to survive. "My" Kevin had disappeared. A young man who constantly struggled with an invisible disability and agonizing chronic pain took his place. Yet still, he was my son, and I would—and tried—to do everything in my power for him. Ultimately, though, we came to a slow, dawning realization there would be "no going back," there would be no more "normal." It was foreshadowing at its finest; after Kevin's death, there was no going back. There was no more normal. I had been picking up our pieces and gluing our lives together again and again with gold for years before I'd had to, one last time, remake our shattered lives after his death.

Grief, I learned, isn't about the single event of that individual dying. There's often something more preceding death—an illness, an injury, sudden or slow—that's going to impact and affect what comes after death. It's a layer of grief I hadn't been aware of; we're coping with complex emotions on multiple different levels, and this understanding—that grief is more than just the moment of death, that there is a whole, complicated backstory to death—is the road to compassion, the path to empathy.

There is an in-between after a loss of this kind. You live in the middle of two worlds, heaven and earth. When I'm with my friends, I'm both down here with them, yet also up there with Kevin. Both/and, I'm both conscious of my loss and surrounded by the feeling I'm here. I no longer have to live in the stark reality that "Kevin died; Kevin died." I have absorbed the reality into my being, into my identity. I am a bereaved mom, no matter how much I wanted to deny it the first time I tried to go through the door of the Bereaved Moms group, and that acceptance, that acknowledgement has been really powerful for me.

It's what led me to my revelation when I made my collage—that I now can see joy in a beautiful butterfly with an amazing design covering its wings. Or a hummingbird close by searching for nectar. Or the beautiful roses in my garden. Now, I love to get up every day, look outside, and see my beautiful blue pots containing different trees, and the flowers all around my yard. It gives me a sense of peace. I feel Kevin's presence with me as I sit on my back patio.

Because I got up.

———

I am left with a beautiful gift from Kevin. A card he wrote me for my birthday. It was a few years before he died.

Ma,

It's tough getting all the appreciation and love I have for you to paper. I will never forget all the sacrifices you made for me. You went without so I could go to basketball camp or have a pair of Jordan's. You researched activities I'd like and supported me in pursuing my dreams.

Thank you for all the energy, rides to practice and school.

Please don't have any regrets about your parenting. I am now seeing what a challenge it is!! I know you tried your best.

Thank you and I love you,

Kevin

It's almost like he knew I would need this, like I would need to be reminded of his appreciation and gratitude when he's no longer here to tell me himself. It is a gift I treasure. It's a reminder of just how loving and kind he was. And, more importantly, it's a reminder that though Kevin may be gone, it's a symbol of the meaning and value of his life, a symbol of what remains: love.

Acknowledgments

One thing I have learned in writing this book is that it takes a village. I'm grateful for my village.

First, I appreciate Clary Tepper, PhD, for encouraging me to write a book about Kevin's story. I didn't believe it was a possibility at the time. Thank you for believing in me.

The She Center, especially my coach, Jillian—thank you for supporting me in my future celebrations. Jillian, you kept me focused on positivity and encouraged me so much on this journey.

Jen Braaksma, my first book coach, you taught me how to write a memoir, held me accountable to writing my pages, and brought my writing to story. Thank you for your encouragement and for seeing the meaning in my story.

Jeanne Gassman, thank you for your encouragement and edits. It meant so much as I was trying to decide if my book was good enough for publishing.

Jessica Buchanan, I felt like you were placed right in my vision as I pondered the next step with my book. Your commitment at Soul Speak Press to give women a place to share their stories and make a difference in the world spoke to my heart. From our first meeting, I was touched by your deep compassion for my story and my need to tell it. You even shed a few tears as I described my journey. Your editing skills are brilliant! All along the way, you helped me find my voice to tell the story of heartbreaking loss and resilience. Thank you so much for helping me to bring my story to life.

Ilsa Manning, thank you for your skilled edits and your gentle way of offering suggestions and corrections.

Stacia Bissell, thank you for your kind words and support. I wish Kevin and I had someone like you early on. It would have made a world of difference.

My rosary group girlfriends, you have been the light in my darkness. I'm so grateful to have you in my life.

To my husband, John, who did a little editing too. Thank you for listening to me read the manuscript many times and helping me find words when I got stuck. Your support has been an invaluable part of the process.

To Danny, for letting me share difficult parts of your story. Your willingness to be open and vulnerable is so impressive. Now we have two writers in the family!

To Kara who got numerous calls to retell stories about Kevin so I could make sure my details were accurate. You always showed me support and gentleness. It was not easy to relive those moments. Thank you for your love and support!

Matt, you have been the best son-in-law. Thank you for your support.

Lorena, you too shared many details to get the story straight. I hope this story reflects your love for Kevin and our love for you. We have been through so much sorrow together. It created a deep bond between us all. I am forever grateful for the happiness you gave Kevin by having a family together.

To my grandchildren, Jack, Carmen, Ozzie, and Mike. I adore all of you and you inspire me to carry on.

To baby Kevin, I hope you grow up to know about your namesake. He was a special person.

To Mimi. My best friend. You supported me as soon as you found out I was pregnant with Kevin and continued to be a support all along the way. Thanks for being with me through all the joy and all the sorrow.

I love you all.

About the Author

Brenda Daly, PhD, LCSW has more than forty years' experience in clinical social work including work with eating disorders, addiction, codependency, and alcoholic family systems. As a result of the loss of her son, Brenda has become a grief specialist with certifications in Grief Therapy as Meaning Reconstruction and Art-Assisted Grief Therapy as well as being a Grief Educator. Brenda has been a speaker with many local groups on grief as well as speaking at the Bereaved Parents of the USA national conference.

Brenda lives in Northern California with her husband and is close to her children and grandchildren.

Made in the USA
Las Vegas, NV
01 August 2024

93224930R00134